ONE-HOUR MYSTERIES

Written by **Mary Ann Carr**

Illustrated by Elisa Ahlin

Edited by Dianne Draze and Sonsie Conroy

ISBN 1-883055-06-7

Contents

Introduction

Children love mysteries and will enjoy becoming detectives when they discover "who done it" in each of the crimes in this book. Solving robberies, a blackmail, sabotage and murder, student detectives will investigate suspects, their alibis and motives, in addition to a variety of other clues. Each clue will provide evidence necessary to eliminate the suspects one by one until the guilty culprit is found. In addition to using deductive reasoning skills, the students will take notes, organize data, and analyze evidence in a classroom forensic lab.

There are five mysteries in this book, each one providing an opportunity to build thinking skills in a motivating context. Each mystery includes complete instructions for the teacher and attractive reproducible pages that outline the mystery and supply clues, one by one until the culprit is found.

- **Mystery at the Mall** takes students to a shopping mall where they will use information obtained by doing deductive logic puzzles to uncover the student who stole the teacher's giant cookie. In addition to introducing deductive logic, this mystery requires students to determine relevant and nonrelevant information.
- **The Coaster Caper** presents a crime at an amusement center. Students will examine motives, determine the validity of alibis and examine physical evidence to find the person who sabotaged the roller coaster.
- **The Case of Santa's Blackmail** takes students to the North Pole to find out which disgruntled employee is threatening to destroy Christmas. Again students will judge motives, consider alibis, and conduct a forensic lab experiment to find the culprit.
- **The Case of the Missing Tiara** takes place in a swank hotel where one of the guests has had her tiara stolen from the hotel safe. The suspects are all employees of the hotel and students must review the motives and alibis as well as perform an experiment to find the crook.
- **A Hollywood Mystery** begins with the announcement that a famous Hollywood director has been found dead. There are many suspects in this mystery and students will have to use all the detective skills they have developed in the other mysteries to solve this puzzler.

This book may be used in a variety of ways. One or all of the crimes may be included in a unit on mysteries. You may also choose to solve a mystery every six weeks. Each mystery requires between 1 - 3 hours depending on the lab analysis, length of the discussions, and student involvement. Though there is no particular order in which the crimes should be solved, it is recommended that the **Mystery at the Mall** be completed first. This particular crime involves matrix logic puzzles, an excellent way to introduce students to deductive reasoning.

While your students will find these mysteries very motivating, you will be pleased with the many reading and thinking skills they will acquire as they try to find the one guilty person in each scenario. Happy Sleuthing!

A Mystery at the Mall

Teacher's Guide

In this mystery students will solve matrix logic puzzles to determine clues that are important in solving the crime. In addition, they will review the statements made by a variety of witnesses who claimed to have seen the culprit at the mall. Only six of the fourteen witnesses are reliable; that is, their statements match up with the evidence obtained from the solution of the logic puzzles. The students will determine which statements are valid and, therefore, which suspect is the culprit.

1. Introduce the Mystery

Begin the mystery by explaining to students that a crime was recently committed at a shopping mall.

Hand out "A Mystery at the Mall" (page 9). After students have read the page, tell them they are going to solve the crime and, just as detectives do, they must begin taking notes as they uncover pertinent facts.

Instruct them to make the following chart:

What ____________________
When ____________________
Where ____________________
How ____________________
Who ____________________
Why ____________________

Have them complete the What? When? and Where? on their chart. Discuss their knowledge of the crime at this point. Explain that as they get more information, they should record it on the chart.

Ask students who they think might be likely suspects. They will probably suggest students from the 6th period class. Explain that even though many people could have committed the crime, it is illogical to think that just anyone would have stolen the cookie considering these facts: the cookie was not valuable (only $15.00), the risk would be great running from the scene with an enormous cookie that would be difficult to hide. The thief, therefore, more than likely had a motive other than obtaining the cookie — a motive that would have made it worth the risk of being caught. Discuss the motive the students in 6th period might have had.

2. Suspects and Alibis

Tell students that when solving a crime, detectives always look for the most logical solution. Explain that in order to practice thinking logically the way a detective does, they will solve a variety of logic puzzles. These puzzles are somewhat like mysteries themselves, in that they require making deductions utilizing a variety of clues. Explain that the solution to each puzzle will provide information pertinent to the case and will help them determine which suspect is guilty.

Hand out the matrix logic puzzle entitled "Suspects and Alibis" (page 10).Discuss what an alibi is. Explain that by solving this puzzle, they will determine how many students in the 6th period class did not have an alibi.

Answers:

One student was suspended.
Two students had play practice.
Three students were cheerleaders.
Four students had no alibis.
Five students had band practice.
Six students played football.

3. Information About Grades

Tell students that now they will find out information about the four students with no alibi. Hand out the logic puzzle entitles "Suspects' Names and Grades" (page 11).

Complete the puzzle and discuss the results.

Answers:

Molly Oswald received a D-.
Otis Snodgrass received an F.
Norman Mitchell received a D.
Samantha Nelson received a C.

Tell students that as they uncover facts about the suspects, they will need to keep notes. Suggest they make a chart that lists the names of the suspects across one axis and information about the suspects along another axis. They should begin with a space for recording the suspects' grades and last names. They will be adding spaces for additional information to the chart, so it should be made so that there is room for a total of eight types of information about the four suspects.

3. Information About Grades

Suspects	*M*	*O*	*N*	*S*
Grade	*D-*	*F*	*D*	*C*
Last name				

Complete the chart with the information available so far.

4. Time Clues

Tell students that now they will find out at what time the students arrived home the afternoon of the crime and also how quickly they could have gotten to the mall on foot.

Hand out the third logic puzzle, "Time Clues" (page 12). Complete the puzzle.

Answers:

Molly - 3:30 p.m., 10 minutes to the mall
Otis - 3:10 p.m., 30 minutes to the mall
Norman - 3:15 p.m., 20 minutes to the mall
Samantha - 3:25 p.m., 15 minutes to the mall

Tell students they should now add two more categories of information to their charts and fill in the information for each of the four suspects.

Suspects	*M*	*O*	*N*	*S*
Last name				
Grade				
Time to home				
Time to mall				

Ask which suspects could have gotten to the mall by 4:00 p.m. on the afternoon of the crime when Miss Wink picked up the cookie. Students should deduce that all of the four students could have made it.

5. Physical Descriptions

Tell students that with the next logic puzzle they will determine the height of each suspect and their hair color.

Hand out the fourth logic puzzle "Description of the Suspects" (page 13). Complete the puzzle.

Answers:

Molly - 5'1", red
Otis - 5'10", brown
Norman - 5'5", black
Samantha - 4'8", blonde

Tell students they should now add the this information to their chart.

Suspects	*M*	*O*	*N*	*S*
Last name				
Grades				
Time to Home				
Time to Mall				
Height				
Hair				

6. Clothing

With this logic puzzle, students will find out what each of the suspects were wearing the day of the crime. Hand out the fifth logic puzzle "Clothing Worn By the Suspects" (page 14). Complete the puzzle.

Answers:

Molly - blue jean jacket, green plaid shirt
Otis - yellow jacket, brown shirt
Norman - tan trench coat, orange sweatshirt
Samantha - red coat, white shirt

Tell students to add coat and shirt categories to the chart so it looks like this:

Suspects	*M*	*O*	*N*	*S*
Last name				
Grade				
Time to home				
Time to mall				
Height				
Hair				
Coat				
Shirt				

7. Mall Map

Explain to students that in addition to gathering these facts about the suspects, they need to have the following information that was reported to the mall security the evening after the crime. Hand out a map of the mall (pages 17 and 18). Ask students to mark on the map the locations indicated by these facts:

- A yellow jacket was found in the dressing room in the So Comfy Clothing Store.
- Two sections of a large chocolate chip cookie were found in the Have Fun Toy Store. One piece was found in the bin with the beach balls. The other had been kicked beneath a shelf containing baby toys.

Discuss how this information might be helpful in determining who committed the crime.

8. Witnesses

Tell students that the security guard questioned a variety of witnesses, shoppers who claimed to have seen suspicious characters at the mall the afternoon of the crime. Explain to students that they will examine the statements made by each witness. As they do this, they will need to refer to the facts on their chart and compare these facts with the facts found in the witnesses' statements.

Hand out "Witnesses' Statements" (pages 15 and 16). After students have read the statement by each witness, ask them to place the witness's number on the map where he or she supposedly saw the suspect. After all the statements have been read, discuss which statements seem to be relevant based on the facts given and facts known about the suspects.

Answers:

Witness 1 - *not relevant. The young person in the book store was not wearing clothing that matched those known to be worn by the four suspects.*

Witness 2 - *relevant. The young person was wearing a brown shirt, was tall and had brown hair. He was carrying a bag from So Comfy Clothing Store. This all matches facts known about a suspect as well as the fact that a yellow jacket was left in So Comfy Clothing Store.*

Witness 3 - *relevant. The yellow jacket, height and hair color all match the facts known about a suspect; not to mention the cookie in his hand.*

Witness 4 - *not relevant. The young person was wearing a yellow jacket and was tall with brown hair; however, he was heavy. This does not match the other information reported by other witnesses; that is, that the suspect in question was thin.*

Witness 5 - *relevant. The young person was wearing a yellow jacket, had brown hair, was tall and thin. This statement matches with the facts known about the suspect. In addition, it corroborates the facts regarding the yellow jacket found in the dressing room of the So Comfy Clothing Store.*

Witness 6 - *not relevant. The young person was wearing a yellow jacket, had brown hair, but was short and was carrying a package from Jeans'N Wear.*

Witness 7 - *not relevant. The statement does not match the facts known about the suspects.*

Witness 8 - *relevant. The young person was wearing a brown shirt, was tall, thin and had brown hair. In addition, he was carrying a package from the So Comfy Clothing Store.*

Witness 9 - *relevant. The statement matches facts about a suspect, including a yellow package and substantiates Witness 10's statement that he saw a suspect running out of the Sports Center Shop. In addition, it gives another piece of evidence (the baseball cap).*

Witness 10 - *relevant. The young person was wearing a brown shirt, jeans, and a black baseball cap. In addition, he had brown hair, was tall and thin. He also was carrying a white container in addition to a yellow bag.*

Witness 11 - *not relevant. The statement does not match the facts known about the suspects.*

8. Witnesses

Discuss which witnesses' statements were relevant. Explain that often the statements made by witnesses when they are questioned are not accurate. They forget what they saw or they actually don't notice something like clothing, hair color or body build. Tell students that when questioning someone, detectives look for match-ups in both the statements made by other witnesses as well as match-ups with the known facts.

Based on the statements made by the six witnesses with relevant statements, who was the guilty suspect? (Answer: Otis Snodgrass).

9. Conclusion

Using the statements made by the six witnesses, ask students to reconstruct on their maps of the mall what Otis did after he committed the crime.

Answer:

He ran down the mall past the fountain across from the Great Buy Department Store, into the Have Fun Toy Store through the door nearest the southwest mall entrance. He broke the cookie in half, kicked one piece under a shelf and dropped the other into the bin containing beach balls. He then left the toy store, probably through the other entrance, and ran into the So Comfy Clothing Store where he purchased an item using cash. He went into the dressing room and left his yellow jacket. He then left the store, carrying the store's yellow bag with his purchase and headed towards the south entrance to the mall. There, he saw a security guard and headed back into the mall. He went to the Sports Center where he bought a baseball cap then headed towards the pet store. There, he bought fish and carried them out in a small container. He then headed out of the mall through the southeast entrance, past a security guard who was not looking for a young person in a brown shirt, wearing a baseball cap, carrying a yellow bag and a white container filled with fish.

Tell students that based on the statements made by witnesses and the facts known about the suspects, the police went to Otis's home the evening after the crime. When confronted with the evidence, he broke down, saying he was sorry and asking what he could do to apologize to Miss Wink. Miss Wink did not press charges. She did, however, make a contract with Otis that he would stay after school each day and work on another term paper. He completed this task in record time. "You would have received an A if I was giving you a grade," Miss Wink told him. "Let this be a lesson that you are capable of doing excellent work if only you will apply yourself." Miss Wink also pointed out how the prank of stealing the cookie had come to no good. "After all, crime does not pay."

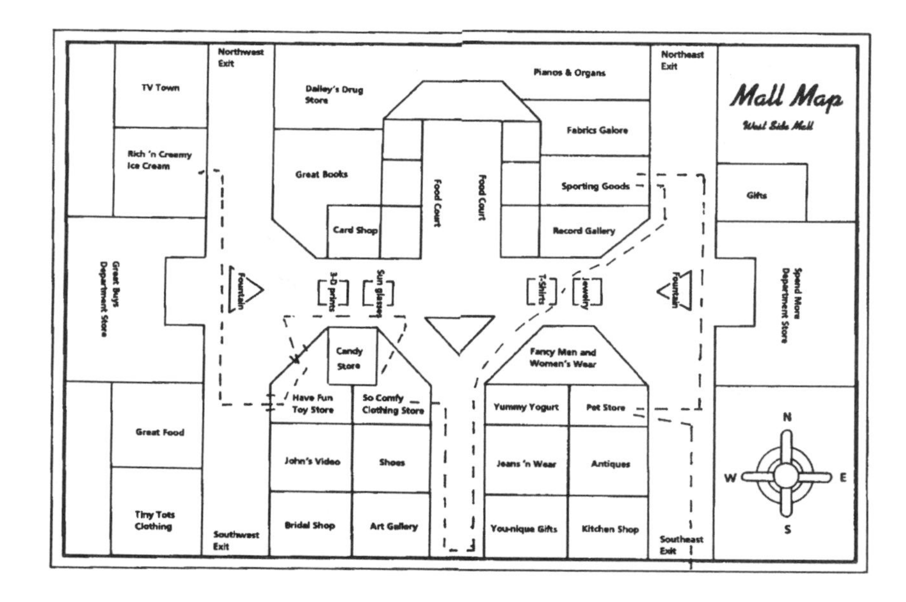

A Mystery at the Mall

Miss Annadale Wink, an eighth grade language arts teacher, was so pleased with the term papers completed by the students in her fifth period class that she decided they needed a special treat. She wanted to surprise the group, however, she could not resist mentioning it later to her sixth period class, explaining that they, too, could have received such a reward if only they had put forth the same effort. "All C's, D's and F's in this class," she had said accusingly. "All A's in my fifth period class."

"This afternoon at four o'clock I am going to the mall to pick up an incredible treat for those wonderful students," she told the sixth period class. "A treat so delicious it is absolutely decadent." She paused, seeming to delight in the students' looks of envy. "A gigantic cookie, more than three feet in diameter, chocolate chip dipped in rich chocolate icing." She paused again, slowly licking her lips. "And of course, ice cream sundaes would be perfect with that. Ice cream and those scrumptious sauces from my favorite place at the mall, The Rich and Creamy Ice Cream Shop."

That afternoon at the mall, Miss Wink picked up the cookie from Mr. Hill's Cookies in the food court. She then went to the ice cream shop where, nodding to the clerk behind the cash register, she placed the cookie on a display of various packages of candy laid out on a wooden table next to the check-out counter. She then followed the clerk to the glass case where the clerk helped her select several flavors of ice cream, allowing her to sample several flavors. While the clerk was filling the cartons with the selected flavors, Miss Wink stepped to a nearby shelf where various sauces and toppings were displayed. Choosing enough for a feast, she headed back towards the check-out counter.

"Oh no!" she exclaimed as she neared the wooden table. The cookie was no longer on the candy display.

She asked the clerk if he had moved it, but the clerk said he had last seen it on the table. "It was the biggest cookie I ever saw," he said. "What could have happened to it?"

"It's been stolen!" Mrs. Wink exclaimed. She spotted a security guard outside the shop. "I've been robbed!" she screamed, racing toward him. She told the guard about the cookie and he immediately called the mall security on a portable phone attached to his belt.

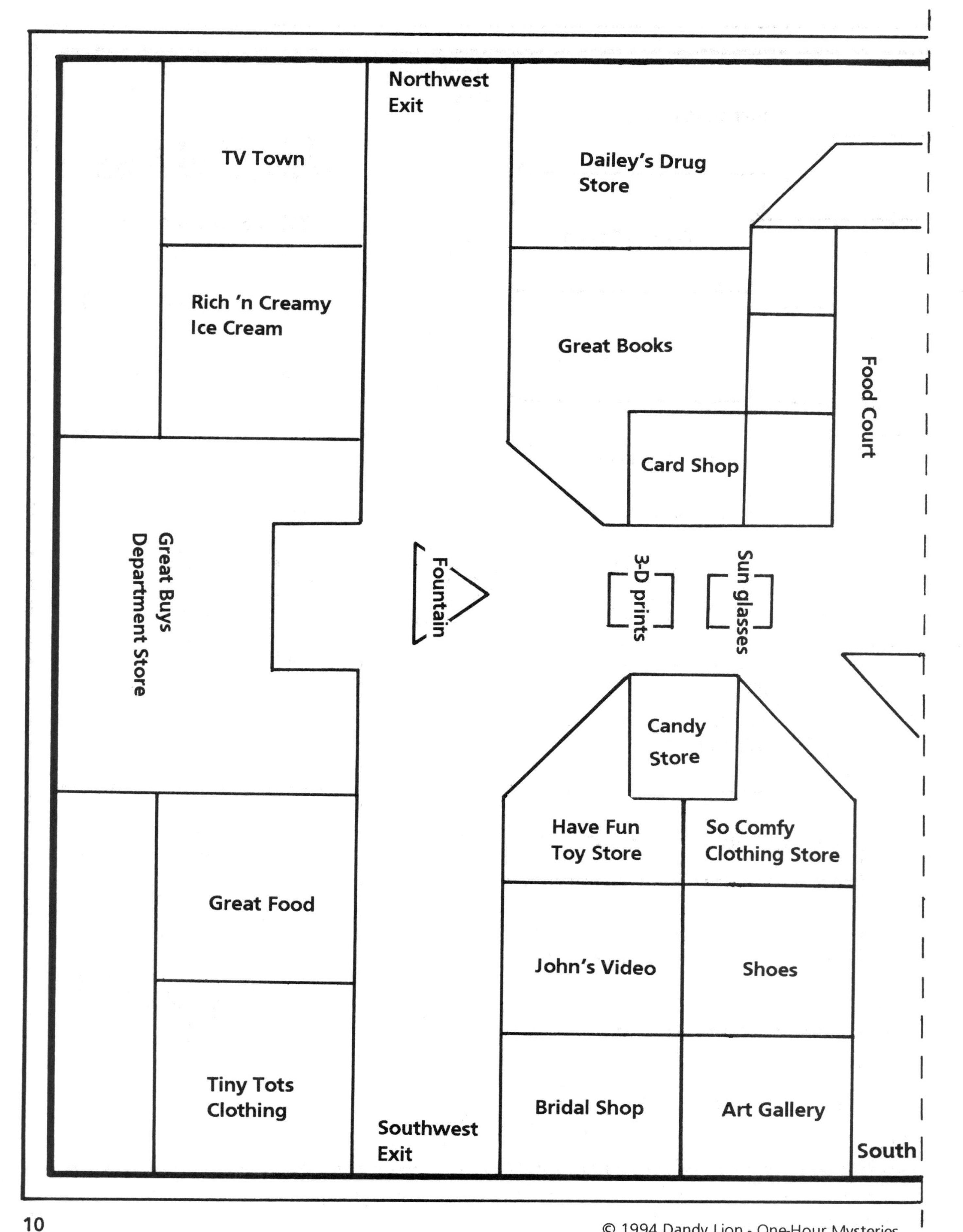
Northwest Exit
TV Town
Dailey's Drug Store
Rich 'n Creamy Ice Cream
Great Books
Food Court
Card Shop
Great Buys Department Store
Fountain
3-D prints
Sun glasses
Candy Store
Have Fun Toy Store
So Comfy Clothing Store
Great Food
John's Video
Shoes
Tiny Tots Clothing
Bridal Shop
Art Gallery
Southwest Exit
South

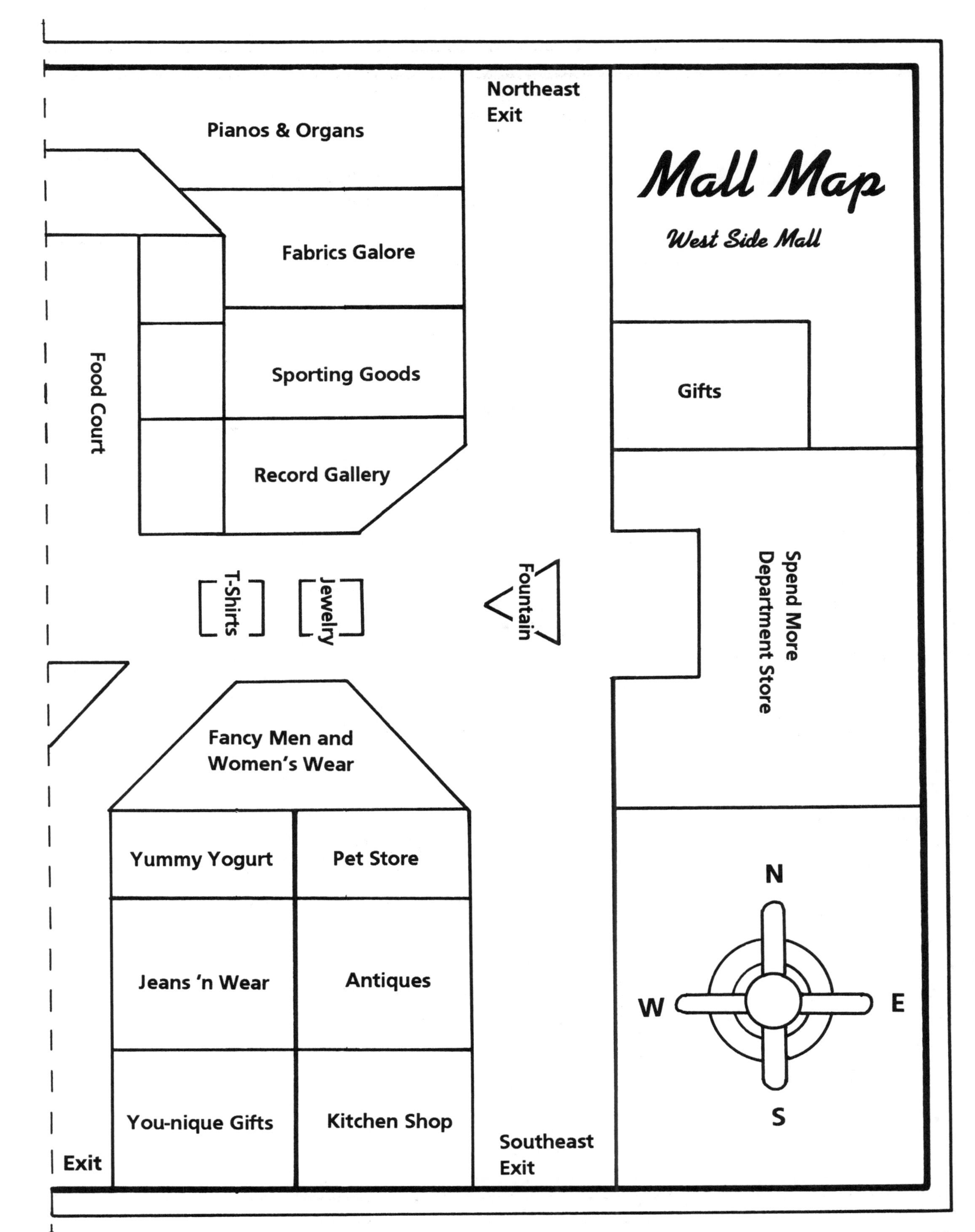

Mall Map
West Side Mall
Pianos & Organs
Northeast Exit
Fabrics Galore
Sporting Goods
Record Gallery
Food Court
Gifts
T-Shirts
Jewelry
Fountain
Spend More Department Store
Fancy Men and Women's Wear
Yummy Yogurt
Pet Store
Jeans 'n Wear
Antiques
You-nique Gifts
Kitchen Shop
Exit
Southeast Exit
N
W
E
S

Suspects and Alibis

Miss Wink was convinced the culprit was a student in her sixth period class. "They were the only ones who knew about my surprise," she stated, "and I'm sure many of those students were not happy about it, especially when I told them that after eating all the sundaes they wanted, the kids in my fifth period class would have free time so they could play their favorite CDs and dance.

Many of the twenty-one students in her 6th period class had alibis. Some of them had remained after school the afternoon of the crime for play practice, band practice, football practice and cheerleading. Each of these activities ended at 4:30 p.m. Some, however, could not account for their whereabouts in the afternoon. Complete the logic puzzle to determine how many students stayed after school for each activity and how many had no alibis.

Clues

1. Only one student was suspended.
2. The number of people at band practice was one less than the number at football practice.
3. The number of students at play practice was two less than the number of students with no alibis and one less than the number of cheerleaders.
4. There were twice as many football players as there were cheerleaders.
5. Twice as many people were at play practice as were suspended.

Number at play practice ____________________

Number at band practice ____________________

Number at football practice ____________________

Number at Cheerleading practice ______________

Number suspended ____________________

Number with no alibi ____________________

Total number **21**

Suspects' Names and Grades

The four suspects who did not have alibis for the afternoon of the crime were Molly, Otis, Norman, and Samantha. Their last names are Mitchell, Oswald, Nelson and Snodgrass. None of the first names begin with the same letter as the last names. Each suspect received either a C, D, D-, or F on his or her term paper. Solve the logic puzzle to find out the last names of each suspect and what grade they received.

Clues

1. The suspect whose last name is Nelson received a C on the paper.
2. Neither Otis or the student who received a D- have last names beginning with M or N.
3. Molly was upset when she received the second to the lowest grade.
4. Norman and the suspect who received an F are friends.

Time Clues

Each of the suspects rode a school bus on the afternoon of the crime and got home at different times. They arrived at 3:10 p.m., 3:15 p.m., 3:25 p.m. and 3:30 p.m. None of the students' parents were at home when they arrived. No one saw the suspects until after 5:00 p.m. that evening. The suspects live in neighborhoods not far from the mall. It takes no more than 10, 15, 20, or 30 minutes to walk to the mall from their homes. Solve the logic puzzle to find out what time each suspect arrived home and how long it would take him or her to walk to the mall.

Clues

1. The suspect who arrived home at 3:10 p.m. could walk to the mall in 30 minutes.
2. Neither Samantha or the student who could walk to the mall in 10 minutes arrived home before 3:20 p.m.
3. Molly arrived home at 3:30 p.m.
4. Otis and the suspect who needed 15 minutes to walk to the mall were friends.
5. It took Norman 20 minutes to walk to the mall.

	3:10 p.m.	*3:15 p.m.*	*3:25 p.m.*	*3:30 p.m.*	*10 minutes*	*15 minutes*	*20 minutes*	*30 minutes*
Molly								
Otis								
Norman								
Samantha								
10 minutes								
15 minutes								
20 minutes								
30 minutes								

Description of the Suspects

The mall security asked Miss Wink for a physical description of the four suspects. She stated that the students had either brown, red, black or blonde hair. No two students had the same color hair. She also told security that the tallest student was 5′10" and the shortest was 4′8". The other two students were 5′1" and 5′5".

"This information is all in their school records," Miss Wink retorted when the security guard asked how she could be so certain about the students' heights.

The guard explained that many witnesses give information that is not exactly factual. "They think they are accurate but frequently they are not. They have forgotten what they have seen or they actually didn't know what they claimed to know."

"Well, I never forget," Miss Wink defended. "After all, I do have a photographic memory. Whatever I see, I always remember." Miss Wink then began giving examples of her amazing memory, recalling not only exact quotes from famous literature but the page number on which each quote could be found in various books.

The guard listened politely for several moments then mentioned to Miss Wink that time was valuable when solving a crime. How quickly can you solve this logic puzzle to find out the height of the suspects and the colors of their hair?

Clues

1. The suspect with blonde hair is shorter than the others.
2. Norman is neither the tallest nor the shortest suspect.
3. Otis has brown hair.
4. The suspect with black hair is 5′5".
5. Molly is 5′1".

Clothing Worn by the Suspects

The security guard asked Miss Wink if she remembered what each of the suspects was wearing that day in school.

"I most certainly do," she said, and she quickly told the guard that the students were wearing a yellow jacket, a blue jean jacket, a red coat and a tan trench coat. They also were wearing a brown shirt, a green plaid shirt, a white shirt, and an orange sweatshirt.

Solve the logic puzzle to find out what color jacket or coat and what color shirt each suspect was wearing.

Clues

1. One suspect wore a white shirt under a red coat.
2. The suspect wearing the trench coat did not wear plaid.
3. Norman does not like red.
4. Otis wore a yellow jacket but not an orange sweatshirt.
5. Molly wore a green plaid shirt.

	yellow jacket	*blue jacket*	*red coat*	*tan trench coat*	*brown shirt*	*green plaid shirt*	*white shirt*	*orange sweatshirt*
Molly								
Otis								
Norman								
Samantha								
brown shirt								
green plaid shirt								
white shirt								
orange sweatshirt								

Witnesses' Statements

Witnesses who claimed to have seen a teenager running in the mall or acting suspiciously were questioned by the mall security. Some of the witnesses were found to be reliable. The statements made by others, however, conflicted with the facts known about the possible suspects.

The witnesses were asked if they had noticed a young person in the mall with a giant cookie or one who was acting suspiciously. They were then asked where they saw the person, what the person was wearing, height, hair color, and if the person was carrying anything.

Read the statements made by each witness. Look for patterns in the statements. For example, did more than one of the witnesses see the same thing? Which statements seem to be relevant? Which do not seem to apply to the crime?

Witness 1

"A young person was in the book store, The Great Books Book Store. He looked suspicious to me, because he was looking through cookbooks. He was wearing a red shirt and red plaid pants. I didn't notice a jacket or anything. He had dark hair; I'm not sure whether it was brown or black. He was average height."

Witness 2

"I was standing in front of the Bridal Shop, waiting for my friend. I saw a boy, a teenager, head straight toward the south entrance. He seemed to be in a hurry, but when he reached the door, he spun around and hurried back down the hallway towards the main part of the mall. I couldn't figure it out until I saw the security guard standing outside the door. That's when I asked the guard if something had happened. The boy was wearing a brown shirt and blue jeans. He was tall, at least 5'9" and skinny, very skinny. I think he had brown hair. He was carrying one of those yellow bags from So Comfy Clothing Store."

Witness 3

"A boy wearing a bright yellow jacket ran past me. I was standing by the fountain in front of the Great Buy Department Store. The boy was carrying the largest cookie I have ever seen. He ran into the toy shop. He was tall with brown hair and lanky; not much meat on his body."

Witness 4

"There was a boy in the gift shop wearing a yellow shirt. He was just looking around, not buying anything. He was tall and heavy, like he had eaten way too many biscuits. He had brown hair. He was not carrying a package or anything."

Witness 5

"When I was waiting to pay for my new sunglasses at the small booth, I noticed a boy running in front of the candy store. He darted into So Comfy Clothing Store. He was wearing a yellow jacket and blue jeans, I think. He had brown hair and was tall, at least 5'9". He was not carrying anything."

Witness 6

"I was shopping in the men's department in the Great Buy Department Store when I noticed a young teenage boy in a yellow jacket looking for shirts. He was short, only about 5'1"or so. He had brown hair. He was carrying a package from Jeans'N Wear."

Witness 7

"I had been looking at Indian jewelry at that booth in the middle of the mall when I saw a teenage girl run into the Fancy Men and Women's Clothing Shop. She acted like she was being chased or something. I looked but saw no one following her. She had on a red shirt. She was tall, like a model, and had incredible hair, blonde and very long.

Witness 8

A young boy almost knocked me down when I was coming out of the Sports Center. He raced past me through the door. He didn't even say 'Excuse Me.' I got a good look at him. He was tall, very thin, and had brown hair. He was wearing a brown shirt and blue jeans. I noticed he had a package from my favorite store, So Comfy Clothing Store."

Witness 9

"I was sitting in front of the Spend More Department Store. I saw a kid walk by wearing a black baseball cap from the Baltimore Orioles. I said something to him as he passed, like 'Good Team,' but he didn't even look up. I was certain he heard me. I figured he didn't want to be bothered with an old man. He was heading down the mall toward the southeast entrance. He was about as tall as my son, 5'10' or so, and skinny like my boy too. His hair was brown. The boy had on a brown shirt and blue jeans and was carrying a package. I think it was yellow.

Witness 10

"I saw a boy coming out of the pet store. He was carrying what I guess was fish in a white container. He also had a yellow bag. I followed him out of the mall, out the southeast entrance. I noticed that he was tall, almost six feet, and skinny. He had on a brown shirt, blue jeans and a baseball cap. I don't know what team, but it was black.

Witness 11

"I was in the kitchen shop when I saw a kid wearing a yellow shirt and a baseball cap come into the store. He wasn't carrying anything, but he did buy a measuring cup that the clerk put in a brown bag. He looked suspicious. I noticed before he actually bought the cup, he was looking at dishes. He glanced around from side to side to see if anyone was watching him. He was tall and rather heavy-set."

The Coaster Caper

Teacher's Guide

1. Introduction

This crime is best presented in the spring when the amusement parks are once again open for the season.

Hand out "The Coaster Caper" (page 20). Read and discuss what facts the student detectives must uncover as they investigate the crime.

After reading this page, fill in the blanks, indicating what crime had been committed, when it was committed and where.

2. The Suspects

Hand out the sheet "Suspect List" (page 21) and discuss it. Fill in the blank at the bottom of the page. Rosco Hepplewhite had no motive. If students argue that he might have wanted a better job, explain that the detectives working on the case thought that he had no logical motive. He stood to lose his raise and promotion if he committed the crime.

3. Suspects' Alibis

Read and discuss the sheet "Suspects' Alibis" (page 22). Who might be questioned to back up or substantiate each alibi? Discuss.

Read and discuss the sheet "Notes to Substantiate the Alibis" (page 23).

Who can be eliminated by his or her alibi? (**Melody Voice**)

4. More Evidence

Read the evidence found in the trash can as described on the sheet "More Evidence" (page 24).

Examine the list of physical characteristics of each suspect.

Who can be eliminated because the clothes wouldn't fit? Which suspect would be conspicuous in the oversized jacket? (**Earline Felldow**n). Remind students that Melody Voice has already been eliminated.

5. Even More Evidence

Read and discuss the sheet "Even More Evidence" (page 25).

Mildred Kerkel has red hair. She can be eliminated based on the fact that a strand of blonde hair was found inside the wig.

Who is the culprit? (**Benny Berleine**)

The Coaster Caper

The Serpentine, the new roller coaster at Wild World Amusement Park, was sabotaged last Sunday. Four wires were cut and two parts were taken from the engine, making the coaster inoperable. After attempting a test run at 9:50 a.m., the Serpentine attendant reported to park officials that something was wrong with the coaster's engine. "The motor will not even turn over," he stated. The crime was discovered when a park mechanic examined the engine.

Notes About the Case

- The Serpentine attendant who operated the coaster Saturday evening told police, "The coaster was running like a jewel all night right up until we closed. There was no indication that anything was wrong at all."
- There was no evidence of a break-in at the park. The employee gate was open at 8:00 a.m. the morning of the crime.

Fill in the important information about the crime as you gather the facts.

What was the crime? ____________________

Where did the crime take place? ____________________

When did the crime take place? ____________________

How was the crime committed? ____________________

Why was the crime committed? ____________________

Who committed the crime? ____________________

Suspect List

Rosco Hepplewhite

42 years old. He is an executive at the amusement park. He was recently promoted and got a $4,000 raise.

Earline Felldown

46 years old. She is the organizer of annual protests against the roller coaster. "They are corrupting our youth," she claimed in last week's newspaper. She has frequently threatened to do something more than protest peacefully.

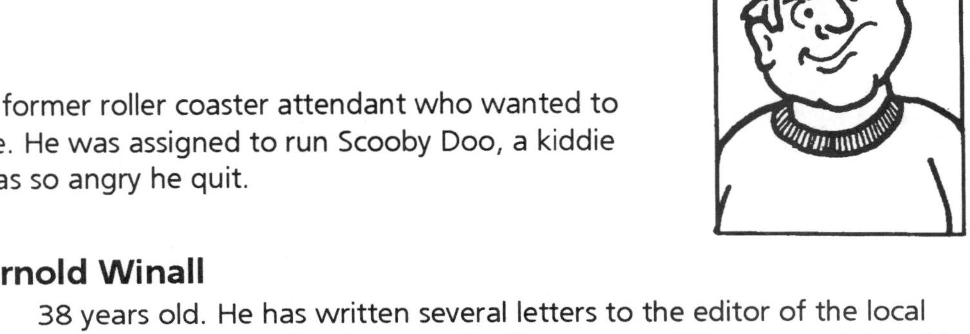

Benny Berleine

20 years old. He was a former roller coaster attendant who wanted to run the new Serpentine. He was assigned to run Scooby Doo, a kiddie coaster, instead and was so angry he quit.

Arnold Winall

38 years old. He has written several letters to the editor of the local newspaper about the dangers of roller coasters. His son was injured in a roller coaster accident in New Jersey.

Mildred Kerkel

21 years old. She is the former attendant on Rebel Yell, another coaster at the Wild World Amusement Park, who was fired for keeping unruly kids on the coaster, making them ride again and again until they cried or got sick.

Melody Voice

20 years old. She is a college student whose boyfriend is a coastaholic. He goes to the park each day it is open and rides the roller coasters over and over. She is always left alone and was reported to have had an argument with her boyfriend in front of the Serpentine last Sunday. She was overheard threatening to do something about the coasters.

Who can be eliminated because they didn't have a motive? ______________________________

Suspects' Alibis

When the suspects were questioned regarding their whereabouts the morning the roller coaster was sabotaged, they gave the following alibis.

Rosco Hepplewhite

"I was in Orlando, Florida at a conference for amusement park officials."

He lives 15 minutes from Wild World Amusement Park.

Earline Felldown

"I was picking up posters at Melda Fry's for a protest that was to begin at 11:00 a.m. in front of the Serpentine.

She lives 20 minutes from Wild World Amusement Park.

Benny Berleine

"I was asleep. I slept until about 12:30 that day."

He lives 30 minutes from Wild World Amusement Park.

Arnold Winall

"I was on the way to the hospital to visit my son."

He lives 20 minutes from Wild World Amusement Park.

Mildred Kerkel

"I was waiting to go shopping with my friend at Potomac Mills."

She lives 10 minutes from Wild World Amusement Park.

Melody Voice

"I was baby-sitting my neighbor's child."

She lives 45 minutes from Wild World Amusement Park.

Notes to Substantiate the Alibis

Rosco Hepplewhite

Rosco was registered at the conference. His attendance was confirmed by three conference leaders.

Earline Felldown

Melda Fry reported that the protest posters were taken from her front porch when she was at church. She left home at 7:30 a.m. for early Mass and didn't return until after 1:00 p.m.

Benny Berleine

Benny's parents were not at home on Sunday. They left at 6:30 a.m. when Benny was asleep to drive to Charlottesville to visit his aunt. They did not return until 9:00 p.m.

Arnold Winall

Arnold arrived at the hospital at 11:00 a.m. The hospital was a 30-minute drive from his house.

Mildred Kerkel

Helen Ross was late getting to Mildred's home for the shopping trip. She didn't get there until 10:30 a.m. She had called Mildred at 7:00 a.m. to say she would be late.

Melody Voice

The neighbor left her child with Melody at 8:30 a.m. She called again at 9:30 a.m. to find out how the child was doing.

Who can be eliminated by their alibi? ______________________________

More Evidence

A paper sack was found in the trash at Wild World Amusement Park that contained the following: a pair of white sweat pants, a navy blue jacket, and a brown wig. A fiber matching the blue in the jacket was found attached to a piece of the Serpentine's engine. The size on the label in the clothing was marked "extra large."

Here are physical descriptions of the suspects. How can this evidence help solve the crime?

Rosco Hepplewhite

5′ 8"	165 lbs.	gray hair	no facial marks

Earline Felldown

5′ 4"	118 lbs.	black hair	mole on the right cheek

Benny Berleine

6′ 3"	215 lbs.	blonde hair	no facial marks

Arnold Winall

6′ 2	235 lbs.	blonde hair	scar on end of his chin

Mildred Kerkel

5′ 11"	173 lbs.	red hair	no facial marks

Melody Voice

5′ 1"	98 lbs.	blonde hair	mole on upper right cheek

Who can be eliminated because the clothes wouldn't fit? ________________________

Even More Evidence

A short strand of blonde hair was found inside the wig. Based on this evidence, who can be eliminated? ______________________________

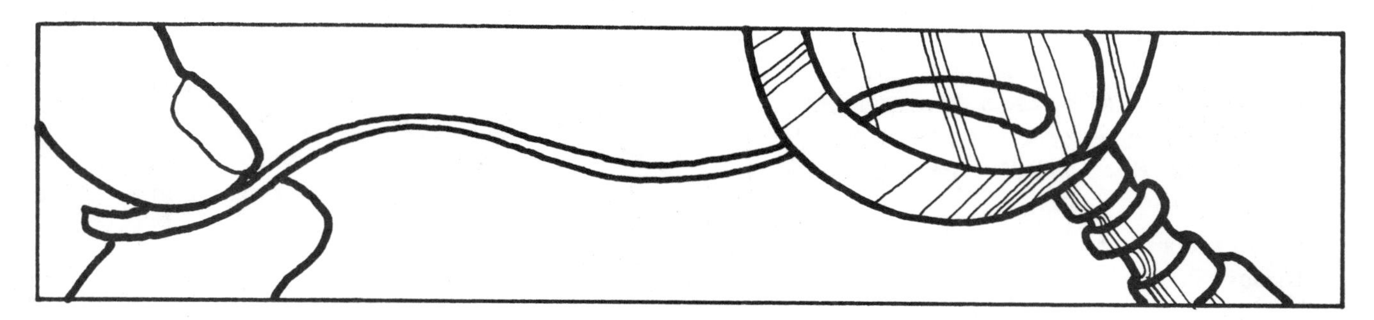

Footprints were found near the Serpentine's engine. They were compared to prints made by the mechanic and attendant, but they did not match their shoes. They were, therefore, thought to belong to the culprit.

The prints were made by athletic shoes. Part of the design looked like this.

Police visited the home of Benny Berleine and Arnold Winall. They asked to examine their closet and found that both men owned athletic shoes. Both of the shoes had dirt on the bottom. Samples of the dirt were taken to the lab where they were to be examined to determine if the dirt was identical to that where the footprint was found.

Which shoe would contain the matching dirt sample? ______________________________

sole of Arnold's shoe

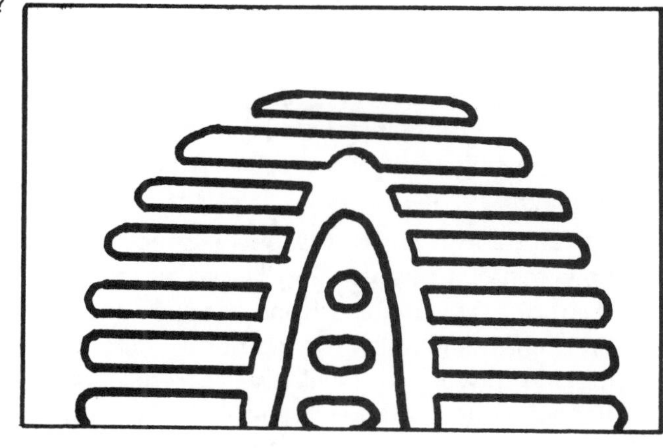

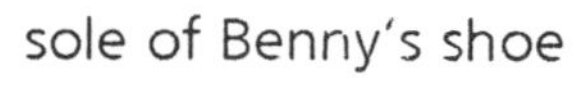

sole of Benny's shoe

Based on this evidence, who is the culprit? ______________________________

The Case of Santa's Blackmail

Teacher's Guide

1. Introduce the Mystery

Grades 3-5:

Tell students that something terrible has happened at the North Pole, something that could ruin Christmas for every child in the world. Explain that Santa had recently announced his plans for reorganization of personnel at the North Pole. Read Santa's "Inter-Pole Memo," (page 30) and discuss.

Read the information about the blackmail notes (pages 28 and 29).

Hand out the "Christmas Gift Requests" (page 31). Ask students to determine if anything is wrong with the list. Discuss their ideas.

Tell students that a second blackmail note was slipped under Santa's door. Read it and discuss. You might want to make a copy of this and the other blackmail note and post them on a bulletin board so you can easily refer to them.

Challenge students to solve the crime and help Santa find the blackmailer.

Grades 6-8:

Give each student a copy of the Introduction, the "Inter-Pole Memo," and the "Christmas Gift Requests." Read all the handouts and then discuss them.

2. Prime Suspects

Explain that detectives questioned 37 elves at the North Pole who were affected by the reorganization. Of these 37, only six were computer literate and capable of this type of sabotage. These six elves are the prime suspects.

Read aloud or handout copies of "Prime Suspects" (pages 32 and 33) and have students read about the suspects silently. Discuss the impact of the reorganization on each suspect and their possible motive or reason for committing the crime.

Ask students if any of these six suspects could be eliminated because they lacked a motive. Point out that Caroling Noel is happy about the reorganizational plan forcing her to retire. She is looking forward to travel. She, therefore, has little motive and can be eliminated from the suspect list. Students might state that she could have been lying and, therefore, could be the culprit. If they argue this, tell them that it is a possibility; however, the detective working on the case considered it to be unlikely in that she had no previous record, was reported by everyone to be devoted to Santa, and had frequently talked about how she would love to travel. For these reasons, the detective crossed her off the list. However, if new evidence is discovered that points to her, she will become a prime suspect once again.

3. Fingerprints

Tell students that the door to Santa's office was dusted for prints. Four prints were found. Hand out copies of "Fingerprints" (page 34) and discuss. Point out that Caroling Noel's prints were not found. This supports her elimination from the suspect list. Also, point out that the fact that Curly Bows's prints were not found does not necessarily mean he had not committed the crime. He could have worn gloves. Because four of the suspect's prints were found on the door, detectives knew no one had wiped the door clean. In addition to the four identified prints, unknown prints were found that were probably Santa's, Mrs. Claus's, or someone they cannot identify.

Ask students if these prints alone would be evidence enough to catch the criminal or convict him or her in court. Discuss their ideas. Point out that the suspect could have visited Santa's office months ago when the plan for reorganization was unknown. A print on a surface such as a door can last for months. Even if the print was recent, the suspect could have gone to the office for reasons that had nothing to do with the blackmail.

Tell students that each suspect was questioned by detectives about their prints found on the door. Read "Statements About Prints" (page 35) and discuss.

Ask students if they think any of the suspects could be eliminated after hearing their statements. Santa's statement supporting Tinsel Green led detectives to eliminate Tinsel from the suspect list. He no longer had a motive. Santa had arranged for him to remain in his same position as toy designer despite the reorganization. The detectives crossed him off the list until such time as additional evidence is found to incriminate him.

4. A Newspaper Clue

Read "A Newspaper Clue" (page 36) and discuss. Ask students who they might question to substantiate these statements. Point out that the only source for the newspaper other than home delivery is the Glacier Newsstand. The owner and only worker at the newsstand could substantiate whether the suspects had purchased a newspaper on the dates described. Read the statements made by the newsstand owner ("Substantiating the Statements," page 37) and discuss. Were any statements substantiated? Could any suspects be eliminated? Students should eliminate Mistletoe and Curly. There was no evidence to support the fact that they had written the blackmail note using cutouts from the newspaper.

5. A Final Clue

The second note Santa received was signed in black ink "DEAD SERIOUS." Using a test, the forensics lab analyzed the note and were able to determine what type of pen the culprit used to write the note. The scientists at the lab used a technique called chromatography. In this procedure the various pigments used in the pen's ink are separated into different color patterns. By examining these patterns, forensic experts can identify the type of pen used in a crime.

Prior to this lesson, you will need to do as follows:

1. Get a black Flair pen and any other type of black small felt-tip marker.
2. Use Bounty towels or any other paper towels (Bounty does work the best) and write the following: DEAD SERIOUS. Write fairly large.
3. On another towel write "Yuley Gooch," using the same black Flair pen as you used to write the words, DEAD SERIOUS. On another towel and, using another brand of felt-tip pen write, "Merry Bells." Explain that these are the signatures used on the time sheet when the suspects signed in for work the day Santa received the blackmail note.

For extension, students can compare a variety of pens. In addition, have them conduct the test using various liquids rather than water. Example: bleach or alcohol. Follow the same procedure for all of the tests.

4. Cut both towels into strips, 1 inch wide and 7 inches long. make sure that writing is on some of the strips.
5. Tape the strips with the most writing onto pencils, allowing the long strip to dangle freely.
6. Gather three plastic cups and water.
7. Label the strips, Exhibit #1 (the words DEAD SERIOUS), Exhibit #2 (Yuley Gooch's signature) and Exhibit #3 (Merry Bells' signature).

Hand out the page entitled "The Final Clue" (page 38). Complete the chromatography test. Discuss the results. With this evidence, you know who committed the crime.

The blackmailer is Yuley Gooch. Detectives made the arrest and Yuley ran his anti-viral program to correct the data. He then fell to the floor at Santa's feet, begging for forgiveness. "Please give me another chance and don't send me to jail," he pleaded. Santa didn't press charges. Instead, he put Yuley to work developing a program to prevent this type of sabotage from ever happening again. Each day Yuley must report his progress to Santa. If he slips behind even one hour in his schedule, Santa has promised to press charges.

The Case of Santa's Blackmail

Detectives at the North Pole Security Agency have requested assistance in the solution of a case that, if not solved, will make this Christmas one every child in the world will want to forget.

The case began when Santa announced his plans for reorganization of personnel the first week in December. Two days after the announcement, he received a note, written in headline letters cut out of a newspaper. The note read:

CANCEL YOUR

REORGANIZATION PLAN

WITHIN 24 HOURS OR

CHRISTMAS WILL BE

RUINED

After reading the letter, Santa was convinced it was nothing more than a prank and tossed it into his bottom desk drawer. Two days later, however, Mr. Dilly, an elf working in the data processing center, approached Santa with a computer printout.

The Case of Santa's Blackmail

page 2

"Something isn't quite right," Mr. Dilly told Santa.

Santa examined the printout that was a list of boys and girls across the United States, their names, ages, requests for toys, and their addresses.

It didn't take long for Santa to realize something was indeed wrong. The list was all mixed up. Children too young to receive chemistry sets and Nintendos had placed them on their Christmas list. Twelve-year olds had written preschool toys on their lists. Children living in Florida had ice skates and sleds on their lists while children living in Kansas and Nebraska had asked for sand buckets and beach balls.

That evening a note was slipped under Santa's door. This note, unlike the other, was printed on a computer. It read,

By now, you know I am serious. The scrambled list is just the beginning. A virus is in your computer. It won't just scramble the data; it will erase all files on December 24. Only I can stop it. I will activate my anti-viral program IF you announce that you will cancel your plan for reorganization.

P.S. If you try to back up your files, the virus will infect the back-up files and erase them the second they are copied back onto another computer.

P.S.S. If you try to fix the data, the virus will activate instantly and erase all the files.

Inter-Pole Memo

To: All Elf Personnel Toy Factory

From: Santa Claus

Date: December 3

Times are hard now for people all over the world. Even those people living in the United States are suffering from a bad recession and children are not asking for as many toys for Christmas as usual. This low demand has forced me to make a difficult decision. Effective January 1 of this new year, I regret that we must cut back in our production. This will require a reorganization of personnel. Unfortunately, lay-offs and early retirements will be necessary for some of you. Many of the remaining personnel will be demoted or reassigned to other divisions at the North Pole.

I realize the hardships this may cause you and your families. It is a necessity, however, if we are to ensure operations in future Christmases.

Details of the reorganization will be posted in each department tomorrow morning.

Christmas Gift Requests: 1993

First Choice Gift Listing

Date of Report: December 5

Name of Child	Sex	Age	First Choice Gift	Delivery Address
Anderson, Dayna A.	F	3	Super Nintendo	Route 1, Box 406, Salisbury NC 28145
Angell, Jerry	M	12	Barbie Doll House	7391 Park Avenue, Springfield VA 22153
Bour, Mike	M	2	Monopoly	316 Well St., Middleboro MA 02346
Bordeaux, Lisa	F	8	Mutant Ninja Turtles	218 Brandon, Bridgewater MA 02333
Carvell, Linda H.	F	11	Buttons N Bells Phone	1524 Honor Dr., Richmond CA 94538
Fox, Mark	M	8	Pretty Lady Makeup Kit	1505 Patricia St., Salt Lake City UT 84032
Gagnon, Susan	F	4	Clue	52 Old Pine Dr., Hanover MA 02341
Holland, Judy	F	2	Game of Life	14304 Cove Ridge Pl., Denver CO 80501
Levine, Arthur	M	10	Little People Garage	111 School St., Kennewick WA 99345
McPherson, David	M	10	Cabbage Patch Kids	83 Bridge St., Monroe LA 72101
Pratt, Lorraine A.	F	6	Battleship	155 Pleasant St., Omaha NE 68891
Sprague, Andy	M	9	Barbie Color Change	106 Lake Dr., Milton DE 19968
Stillwagon, Jose	M	8	Barbie Magical Motorhome	1401 Glade Rd., Blacksburg TX 75772
Stone, Mary	F	10	Nintendo Game	Route 2, Box 441, Oxford MS 38655
Villiard, Robert	M	9	Playskool Busy Driver	508 Old Farm Rd., Franklin ND 56123

Prime Suspects

After talking with Santa and other elf personnel, the detectives found that 37 elves were affected by the cut-backs and reorganization. All were questioned. Of these 37, only 6 were found to be computer literate and capable of the sabotage. These 6 elves are considered the prime suspects.

Mistletoe Kisses

Mistletoe has worked in Customer Service since her recent graduation from the Elf Academy. She was one of four elves responsible for processing all the letters children sent to Santa telling what they wanted for Christmas and entering the data into the computer.

In the reorganization, Mistletoe would be transferred to the Customer Service at the South American field office in Bolivia. Mistletoe was engaged to a young elf who would remain at the North Pole. She had pleaded with her supervisor to let her stay in her present position. "This move will ruin my life," she had told him. "I'll do anything to stay," she had later told a co-worker.

Caroling Noel

Caroling has worked as a doll designer for 132 years. She designed many lines of dolls that had been popular through the years. Caroling had used computers assisted design (CAD) programs in designing her latest doll.

Caroling would have to retire as a result of the reorganization. "I am ready to retire," she told her co-worker. "It will be great. I can finally do those things I've been unable to do all these years, like travel. I've always wanted to see the Bahamas. Now I can do it."

Yuley Gooch

Yuley was a programmer analyst in the Data Processing Department. He loved computers and was the best programmer in the department. He paid no attention to deadlines, however, and was always behind in his work.

One programming position would have to be eliminated in the reorganization. As a result of his poor performance, Yuley was selected by his supervisor to be laid off. He was reportedly very angry. "I'm the only one in this department who really knows what he is doing," he told his supervisor.

Prime Suspects

page 2

Tinsel Green

Tinsel had been a toy designer for forty years. He used computers in creating his toy designs. In addition, he spent hours during his leisure time working on the computer.

Recently, Santa had rejected each of his designs, stating they were environmentally unsound. His last toy had angered Santa.

"You know aerosol sprays damage the ozone layer," Santa was heard counseling Tinsel. "The gun you designed works on the same principle." He was then heard chiding Tinsel for not having a conscience about the environment. It was no surprise when the reorganization resulted in his demotion.

Curly Bows

Curly had been a top executive for Santa for 60 years. The divisions under his supervision included Data Processing, Customer Service, Accounts Receivable and Accounts Payable.

The reorganization grouped his divisions under Product Development and his position was downgraded accordingly. He was scheduled to be manager of Data Processing.

"Whoever's responsible for this reorganization plan certainly ought to pay!" he retorted to a systems analyst who would work for him in Data Processing.

Merry Bells

Merry had worked in Public Relations for 120 years. She had been responsible for much of Santa's popularity. She had come up with the campaign that placed Santa's helpers in every department store in the country and had arranged to have Santa appear each year in the Macy's Thanksgiving Day Parade. Those ideas had been brilliant ones, but Merry had not come up with a good idea in recent years. She was negative about the younger elves' ideas, always saying "That would never work."

As a result of the reorganization, Merry would be given a year's sabbatical. She would be required to take courses at the Elf Collegiate Academy to update her credentials for her current job.

"How could Santa do this?" she had asked angrily. "Without me, he'd mean no more to the world than candy corn at Halloween."

Fingerprints

Because the first note was slipped under the door to Santa's office, detectives dusted the door for fingerprints. The following prints were found. Examine them carefully to determine if any of the prints match the suspects' prints.

Suspects' Prints

Merry Bells

Curly Bows

Tinsel Green

Yuley Gooch

Mistletoe Kisses

Caroling Noel

Prints Found on Santa's Door

door knob

right hand edge above door knob

right hand edge below door knob

middle of door even with knob

Statements About Prints

The suspects made the following statements when detectives asked them how their finger prints were found on the door to Santa's office. Read each statement carefully. Can any of these suspects be eliminated from the suspect list?

Mistletoe Kisses

"My fiance and I went to Santa's office to plead with him to let me stay here at the North Pole. I knocked but he wasn't there. We never went back. We lost our nerve."

Santa's secretary was questioned. She stated that she had not seen the young couple, but she said that she was away from her desk most of the week with the flu.

Yuley Gooch

"As soon as I heard I was to be laid off, I went to Santa's office to tell him I was the best programmer he would ever have. Someone else was already with Santa complaining about the reorganization. I admit I eavesdropped and leaned my ear against the door to hear better. I must have touched the door. I left when I heard Santa come towards the door and I never went back."

The secretary had not seen Yuley. "He must have come when I was sick," she said.

Tinsel Green

"I went to Santa's office to apologize about my insensitivity about the environment and to show him my design for the toy gun, eliminating all environmental hazards. He was very pleased and stated he had been too harsh. He told me that he thought I was one of his best designers and he said he was going to arrange it so I could keep my same job and not be demoted."

When questioned, Santa substantiated Tinsel's statement. "He was our best designer," he said. "I lost my temper over his aerosel gun, but when he showed me his new design, I realized we could not afford to demote him. It would be a great loss to millions of children across the world who enjoy his toy designs.

Merry Bells

"I haven't been near Santa's office since his announcement about the reorganization. I used to go to his office frequently to show him my campaign ideas."

Neither Santa or his secretary had seen Merry Bells near his office.

A Newspaper Clue

The first note sent to Santa was written using headlines from newspapers. After examining the note, forensic experts found the headlines to be from two newspapers: The Polar News, dated November 28th and November 30th. Detectives questioned the suspects to find out if they received these particular newspapers and, if so, what they had done with them.

Read the suspects' statements carefully. Then read the statements made by the owner of the Glacier Newsstand, the only source for the newspaper other than home delivery. Can any suspect be eliminated from the suspect list?

Mistletoe Kisses

"I have the paper delivered everyday. Don't get to read it that often, however. I'm just so busy with my boyfriend."

When asked what she did with her old papers, Mistletoe stated she kept them in her cellar. After examining a stack of them, detectives found the two papers in question. Nothing was cut out of either of them.

Yuley Gooch

"I buy papers at the Glacier Newsstand most mornings."
When asked what he did with his old papers, Yuley showed detectives a receipt from the North Pole Recycling Center. "I take them to the center once a week on my way home from the office. I never even bring any home."

Police checked the dates on the receipts and found one marked November 30.

Curly Bows

"I never read the paper. Haven't bought one in years."

Tinsel Green

"I get the Sunday paper delivered. And I buy one at the newsstand about once or twice a week. I throw my old papers out with the trash.

Merry Bells

"I buy the newspaper each morning."

Merry showed detectives the bottom of her hamster cage. *"And that's how I use the old ones,"* she stated. *"Each day I shred them and put it in the cage for little Snowflake."*

Substantiating the Statements

These statements were made by the owner of the Glacier Newsstand when he was questioned as to whether he sold newspapers to any of the suspects.

Mistletoe Kisses

"I have never sold a paper to Mistletoe or her boyfriend," he said. "She always buys those glamour magazines and he buys nothing but candy."

Yuley Gooch

"I sell Yuley a paper just about every day," he stated.

Curly Bows

"Curly never buys a paper. He is only interested in sports, so he buys a sports magazine. I guess he would buy a newspaper if I would sell only the sports section, but I refuse to do that. I guess he gets the latest game scores from the television."

Tinsel Green

"Tinsel frequently buys a paper from me; three or four times a week, it seems. I can't remember exactly when he did and didn't buy a paper."

Merry Bells

"Merry is here early every morning for her paper. She always wants a peppermint stick as well."

Were any of the suspects' statements substantiated? ______________________________

The Final Clue

The signature on the second note, DEAD SERIOUS, was printed in black ink. Using a chromatography test, the experts at the forensic lab analyzed the note and were able to determine what type of pen the culprit used to write the letters. The scientists at the lab used a technique called chromatography. In this procedure, the various pigments used in the pen's ink are separated into different color patterns. By examining these patterns, forensic experts can identify the type of pen used in a crime.

The ink in the pen used to write the blackmail note was compared to the pen used by the two suspects when they signed their name on the time cards the day Santa received the note.

Use the following procedures to analyze writing samples and determine who wrote the blackmail note.

The Chromatography Test

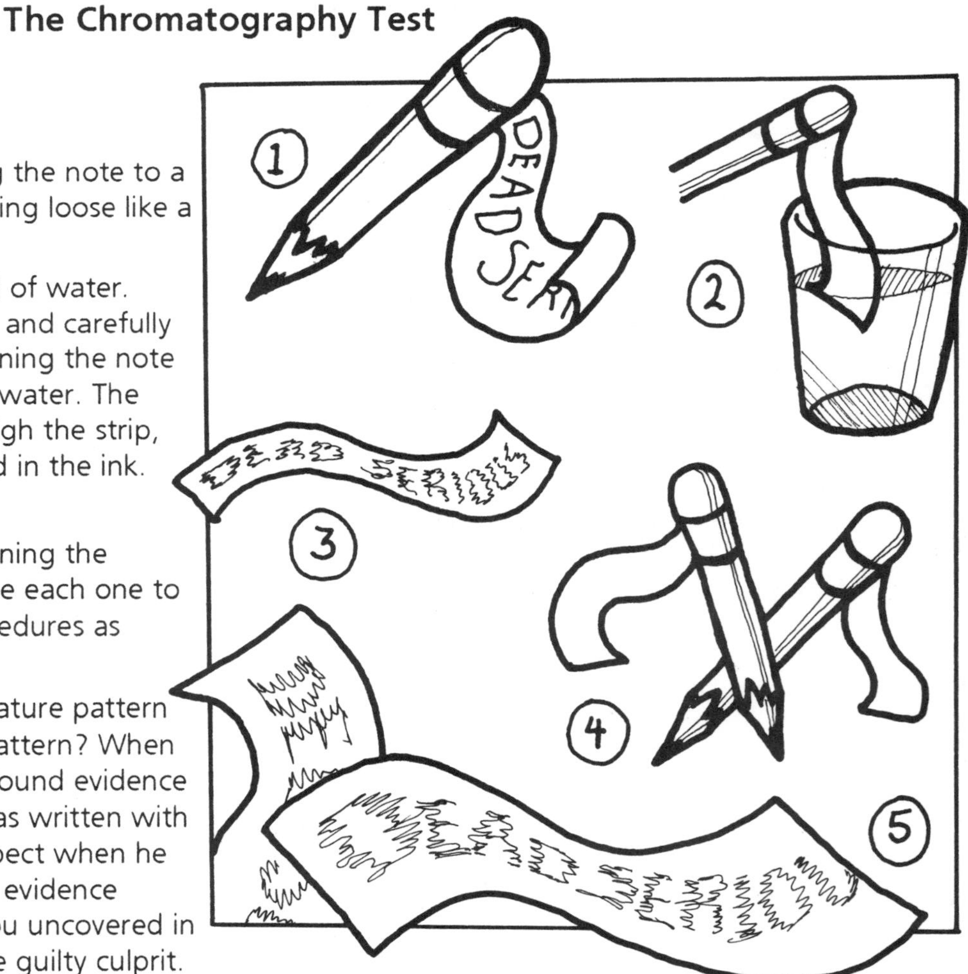

1. Tape a strip of paper containing the note to a pencil or straw, the strip dangling loose like a flag on a pole.
2. Fill a plastic cup one quarter full of water. Place the pencil above the cup and carefully lower the strip of paper containing the note until the end of it touches the water. The water will quickly rise up through the strip, separating the substances used in the ink.
3. Allow the strip to dry.
4. Now, take the two strips containing the names of the suspects and tape each one to a pencil. Follow the same procedures as above.
5. Compare the strips. Which signature pattern matches the DEAD SERIOUS pattern? When you determine this, you have found evidence to prove the blackmail note was written with the same pen used by the suspect when he or she signed in for work. This evidence combined with all the other you uncovered in your investigation points to the guilty culprit.

Who is the guilty person? ______________________________________

The Case of the Missing Tiara

Teacher's Guide

1. The Introduction

Hand out copies of "The Case of the Missing Tiara." (page 41). Read and discuss the information.

Write the following questions on the blackboard or on a poster:

What?
Who?
Where?
Why?
When?
How?

As facts are gathered, fill in information about each question. Students will be able to refer to these facts as needed throughout the case.

2. The Suspects

Hand out copies of "List of Possible Suspects" (page 42). Read the sheet and discuss the suspects. Which suspects have a motive? Can any suspects be eliminated from the suspect list because of lack of motive? The manager and the night security guard have no motive or reason to commit the crime. If students argue that they do, point out that the manager could hurt his position by committing the crime and would gain nothing. State that the detective working on the case eliminated them for the time being because there was no logical motive. However, if evidence is uncovered that points to either of the two, they would be placed back on the suspect list.

3. The Alibis

Hand out copies of "Suspects 'Alibis" (page 43). Read the sheet. Discuss the alibis and who should be questioned in order to substantiate these alibis.

Hand out "Notes Regarding Alibis" (page 44). Read the notes that were written by the detective on the case and discuss them. Are any of the alibis substantiated? Why and why not?

Can any suspects be eliminated because their alibis were substantiated? The manager, night security guard and the maid's alibis were substantiated.

4. Chemical Evidence

Prior to this lesson, you will need to collect the following materials:

baking soda	powdered sugar
cornstarch	flour
vinegar	iodine
a small candle	tin foil
wooden clothes pins	plastic spoons
paper towels	plastic bags

This lesson can be done as a demonstration or with small groups of students testing the powders. Follow the directions on the page entitled Chemical Evidence (page 45) for steps to analyze the powders. Each of the powders should be **numbered** as follows (do not label the bag, identifying the type of powder):

1 - baking soda *(found on the day clerk's shoes)*

2 - powdered sugar *(found on the night clerk's shoes)*

3 - powdered sugar *(found on the chef's shoes)*

4 - cornstarch *(found on the chef's shoes)*

5 - flour *(found on the chef's shoes)*

The powder found at the crime scene should be placed in another bag and labeled Exhibit A. **(This powder is powdered sugar).**

Test this powder. Ask students which powders reacted like this one did.

Note:

Baking soda will fizz when in contact with vinegar. The acid in the vinegar reacts with the carbonate in the soda to produce carbon dioxide. The other powders will not be affected by vinegar.

Starch will turn blue-black when in contact with iodine. The other powders are not affected by iodine.

Sugar will caramelize when heated. The others will not.

Read and discuss the information on the handout. What suspects can be eliminated given this evidence? (day desk clerk can be eliminated because the powder found on his shoes was baking soda.)

The powder found at the crime scene was powdered sugar. This same powder was found on the night clerk's shoes and the chef's shoes.

5. A Typewriter Clue

Read or hand out copies of "A Typewriter Clue" (page 46) and discuss the evidence. Explain that though both the day and night clerk could have had the opportunity to write the note left in the safe, the evidence points to **Brevard Muldane.**

Tell students that Brevard Muldane was arrested and taken down to police headquarters. He confessed to the crime.

The Case of the Missing Tiara

Countess Tiganello, visiting our country from Italy, stopped in Washington for a two-day layover in order to visit her aunt. A frequent visitor to the city, the Countess always stayed at the Byson's Corner Palace Ritz. "They treat me like a queen," she stated.

She was horrified to learn that her precious diamond tiara, valued at $250,000, was stolen from the safe at the hotel only one and a half hours after her arrival on Wednesday, November 18, 1993.

The Countess checked into the hotel at 3:20 p.m. on that date. The tiara and a diamond brooch were placed in the safe located in the hotel manager's office ten minutes later at 3:30 p.m. At 5:00 p.m. the Countess called the manager, requesting that he bring the brooch to her room so she might wear it when dining with her aunt. At that time, the manager discovered the tiara was missing.

Additional Facts

- The safe was locked using a combination. The manager was the only one at the hotel who knew the combination. There was no evidence of forced entry into the safe and no fingerprints were found.
- A copy of the combination was locked in the manager's desk in the bottom left-hand drawer. The manager kept the key to the drawer in his briefcase, which he always kept in his office. The key was missing two weeks ago for about 3 hours between 3:30 p.m. and 6:00 p.m.
- "I frequently leave my office during the day," the manager stated. "I close the door but I never lock it."
- The Countess reserved her room three weeks ago. Only six people at the hotel and her aunt knew of her plans to visit Washington. These hotel employees included the manager, the day desk clerk, the night desk clerk, the night security guard, the chef at the hotel's restaurant, and the penthouse maid.
- A typewritten note was found in the safe. It read, "The rich get richer no more." No prints were found on the note.

List of Possible Suspects

Hotel Manager - Theodore Hopson

45 years old. He has worked for the hotel for 15 years. He was chosen "Manager of the Year" at the annual Palace Ritz Incorporated meeting held in August.

Day Desk Clerk - Mary Dell Brimstone

25 years old. She has worked for the hotel for 2 years. She loves to read about famous people, particularly the royal family. She frequently reads the national tabloid newspapers and discusses the latest gossip about royal family members. She had stated to the first floor maid that she wished that she had been born into royalty so she could have all the luxuries.

Night Desk Clerk - Brevard Meldane

30 years old. He has worked for the hotel for 2 months. He loves to spend money. He drives a BMW. He frequently talks about his latest purchase and recently confessed to a hotel waitress that he had 14 charge cards.

Night Security Guard - Nelson Painter

60 years old. He has worked for the hotel for 5 years. He is a retired policeman. Last year he won three million dollars in the lottery, but he continues to work.

Chef - Justin Aber

24 years old. He has worked for the hotel for 6 months. He was trained as chef at Brenda's in New Orleans. He wanted to work at an overseas Palace Ritz but had been told when he was hired he wasn't quite good enough. He frequently told waitresses that Palace Ritz was going to be sorry one day for not recognizing his talents.

Penthouse Maid - Natasha McNeeley

44 years old. She worked for the hotel for 4 years. She is a single parent with one daughter, a talented gymnast. She had wanted her daughter to train under an Olympic coach but could not afford the cost. She had frequently talked to the other maids about her wish to be a better provider for her daughter.

Suspects' Alibis

Manager

- He was on duty on the day of the crime from 9:00 a.m. to 6:00 p.m.

"After I placed the tiara and brooch in the safe I was out of my office until 5:00 p.m. when the Countess called. I was in the ballroom meeting with a man from the Bowl-Over Clown Alley, planning a March conference."

Day Desk Clerk

- She was on duty from 8:00 a.m. to 4:00 p.m.

"I left the hotel promptly at 4:00 p.m. and went to Byson's Corner to meet my friend, Mildred Rugg."

Night Desk Clerk

- He was on duty from 4:00 p.m. to 12:00 a.m.

"I got to work at 3:55 p.m. and worked at the desk as usual."

Night Security Guard

- He was on duty from 12:00 midnight to 8:00 a.m.

"I was at home, sitting on my front porch from about 3:00 p.m. to 5:30 p.m., talking to my neighbor."

Chef

- He was on duty from 4:00 p.m. to 11:00 p.m.

"I got to work at 4:05 p.m. and immediately began preparing my special sauce, one that is exquisite, for Steak Diane."

Maid

- She was on duty from 9:00 a.m. to 4:00 p.m.

"I was training a new girl all afternoon from 1:00 p.m. on. The first floor maid finished early and helped us. We were done at 3:30 p.m. and sat in the maid's room until 4:30 p.m. drinking coffee. Then I left and picked up my daughter at the baby-sitter's at 4:45 p.m."

Notes Regarding the Alibis

Manager

- The clown from the Bowl-Over Alley stated that he had talked with the manager in the ballroom from about 3:30 p.m. to just a few minutes before 5:30 p.m."

Day Desk Clerk

- Mildred Rugg told detectives she had been detained at the dentist and didn't get to Byson's Corner until 5:45 p.m.

Night Desk Clerk

- Several hotel guests stated they had seen the clerk at the front desk.
- The guest in room 135 told detectives she had come to the desk at 4:30 p.m. to get directions to the Smithsonian. The clerk was away from the desk. She waited for 5 minutes and grew impatient when the clerk didn't come and went back to her room.

Night Security Guard

- The next door neighbor stated that he and Nelson had argued about politics while sitting on the porch.

Chef

- No one saw the chef until 5:00 p.m. when the waitresses came to work.

Maid

- The 1st floor maid stated she had helped Earline and the new employee after 2:30 p.m. and had talked until 4:30 p.m.
- The new maid told detectives she had started at 1:00 p.m. and Earline had worked with her all afternoon, showing her what to do. They all left at 4:30 p.m.
- The baby-sitter had talked with Earline for about 5 minutes.
- The hotel was a 15 minute drive from the baby-sitter's home.

Chemical Evidence

When the manager's office was closely examined by forensic experts, traces of a white powder were found on the floor just below the safe. Some of the powder had smudged on the carpet and, under close examination, a slight impression of a shoe was found. With this evidence, the detectives examined the suspects' shoes. Traces of a white powder were found on the sides of each shoe. The powders found were taken to the lab and analyzed.

Using the directions below, analyze the five different types of powders found on the shoes. Then run an analysis on the powder that was found at the crime scene. If the powders match up, the evidence will help identify the guilty culprit.

Powder 1 was found on the Day Desk Clerk's shoe.

Powder 2 was found on both the Night Clerk's shoe.

Powders 3, **4** and **5** were found on the Chef's shoes.

How to Analyze the Powders

1. Get six pieces of paper and cut each piece in half. Lay five of the pieces on the table and label them *powder 1, 2, 3, 4*, and 5. Label the sixth piece *exhibit A* and put it to one side for now. Then put a sample of each of the five powders on the respective pieces of paper.
2. Take the other six pieces of paper and also label them *powder 1, 2, 3, 4* and *5,* and *exhibit A.* These will be your data sheets for recording the results of the experiments. Staple them together.
3. Examine each of the five powders closely with a hand lens. Record your observations on the corresponding data sheets.
4. Put a drop of vinegar on a small sample of each powder. Record what happens to each substance on your data sheets.
5. Put a drop of iodine on a sample of the powders. Record what happens.
6. Heat each of the powders using a small foil bowl held with a wooden clothes pin. Record what happens.
7. Get a sample of the powder found at the crime scene. Put it on the piece of paper labeled *exhibit A*. Follow the same procedures as above. Record the results.
8. Now, compare the data. Did any of the powders found on the suspects' shoes react to the tests the same way as the powder found at the scene of the crime?

Who can be eliminated because of this chemical evidence? ______________________

A Typewriter Clue

The note found in the safe was typed. After carefully examining the note, forensic experts determined that the note was written on a Speedy-Type typewriter.

Detectives then questioned the suspects and asked to see their typewriters.

Three suspects used typewriters in their offices. A Speedy-Type was at the front desk and was used by both the night desk clerk and the day desk clerk. Justin Aber used a Speedy-Type in his office in the kitchen to record various recipes and to fill out his order forms. Detectives typed the note found in the safe on both of the two Speedy-Type machines. These notes were then analyzed by experts. Examine the original note found in the safe. Do any of the notes written on the suspects' typewriters match the original?

Original Note

The rich get richer no more.

Sample 1 - typewriter in the kitchen

The rich get richer no more.

Sample 2 - typewriter at the front desk

The rich get richer no more.

Who stole the tiara?____

A Hollywood Crime

Teacher's Guide

1. Introduction

The Hollywood crime is a murder mystery and is appropriate for grades 6-8. In solving this crime, students are first given evidence that incriminates a particular suspect. They will draw conclusions based on this evidence. The case, however, is not solved, as the students will find out, when new evidence is uncovered. They will then consider new suspects and will continue to uncover evidence until the crime is solved.

Tell students a crime was recently committed in Hollywood. John Parker, the detective on the case, sent his notes to challenge the students to solve the case using the evidence he had uncovered in his investigation. He would like to know if the students could solve the case if they were given evidence the way it was presented to him.

Hand out "A Hollywood Crime" (page 50). Ask students to read the newspaper article. After they have read it, discuss the article.

Ask them to read Detective Parker's notes regarding facts about the case (pages 50 and 51). Discuss the notes and have students complete their own notes about the case on the bottom of the second page.

Explain to the students that they will be referring to Parker's notes, but as student detectives, they will keep notes of their own pertaining to the case.

There will typically be a variety of responses to the questions, "Who might have done it?" Students might present the case that it was the night security guard because he was the person who discovered the murder. Explain that although that is a possibility, it is highly unlikely. Provide the following facts about the night security guard.

Night Security Guard - age 47. Jonesburg has worked for Van Harsky for 20 years. He is grateful to his employer not only for his excellent salary but also because Van Harsky hired several members of Jonesburg's family to work at the studio when they were unable to find work elsewhere.

Explain that detectives would consider the security guard an unlikely suspect. He had no motive. In addition, because it was customary for Van Harsky and Mrs. Thornwell to have tea together, it would have been almost impossible for the guard to slip the poison in the teapot while she was in the office.

Students might suggest that Van Harsky committed suicide. Explain the following information about the victim:

One of Van Harsky's films had won an Academy Award last year for Best Picture. Another of his films was considered a shoo-in for a nomination this year.

Van Harsky was quoted as saying, "These are the best years of my life. I have my health, success, friends, and a sense of peace. What else could a person want?"

Explain that detectives would consider it unlikely that Van Harsky would have committed suicide. If he had killed himself, he probably would not have chosen to do it in this manner, drinking tea with his secretary.

Explain that detectives consider first what is most likely to have happened. Discuss who would be the most likely suspect considering the information found in Parker's notes. Myrtle Thornwell was seen taking tea to Van Harsky. When his body was found, a cup was overturned beside him indicating he had been drinking tea from that cup. Traces of arsenic were found in the tea in the teapot as well as in the two cups. These facts point to Myrtle Thornwell as the prime suspect.

Discuss what Detective Parker would do. Students should suggest that he would question a variety of employees at the studio and gather facts regarding Myrtle Thornwell.

2. A Prime Suspect

Hand out Parker's notes regarding facts about Myrtle Thornwell and his notes on the follow-up questioning (page 52). Ask students to read Parker's notes then complete their own notes on the case.

2. A Prime Suspect, continued

Discuss their notes. Tell them what they have written down is only an assumption. Based on the evidence, it might be easy to assume that Thornwell committed the crime. She was heading towards his office; she had a pot of tea, and she had a motive. Explain that an **assumption** is an inference based on current facts and past experience. There are two types of assumptions. A **valid assumption** is one that is based on sufficient facts to support the inference. A **false assumption** is an assumption that is not based on sufficient facts, but one that has been made by jumping to conclusions. Explain that there are not enough facts in this case so far to make a valid assumption. Warn students that as detectives they must be careful not to jump to conclusions; therefore, they must gather more evidence.

Discuss what Detective Parker would do. He would likely attempt to locate Myrtle Thornwell.

3. A Suspect Is Questioned

Tell students that Myrtle Thornwell's home was under surveillance. The evening after the crime, she was seen arriving at her home in a taxi. Detectives questioned her shortly after her arrival.

Pass out Parker's notes regarding the interview with Myrtle Thornwell (page 53). Ask students to read and complete their notes on the case. Then discuss how this evidence might affect the investigation.

Discuss what Detective Parker would do. He would probably substantiate Thornwell's story by contacting the airline reservations desk, the hospital in Boston and Thornwell's brother.

4. Substantiation

Hand out Parker's notes regarding facts to substantiate Thornwell's statement (page 54). Ask students to read and complete their notes about the case.

Discuss their notes — WHO might have committed the crime and HOW? Students might develop one of the following scenarios:

The culprit called Myrtle Thornwell the night before the crime, pretending to be a nurse. She told Myrtle that Myrtle's brother was sick. Later that evening, she called Van Harsky, pretending to be Myrtle and left a message saying her brother was not sick after all and she would be at work the next day. Discuss what assumptions the culprit had made about Myrtle Thornwell.

The day of the crime the culprit, dressed as Thornwell, arrived at the studio at her regular time. She remained in her office all day, not even going for a coffee break. Discuss why the culprit would have done this.

The culprit later prepared tea and drove a cart to the castle. At some point, it is not known when, the culprit put arsenic in the teapot, served the poisoned tea, and Van Harsky fell to the ground. The culprit waited at the studio until the next morning. Then the culprit, using another disguise, left the studio sometime during the day when many people were entering and leaving the studio. There are many places to hide on the back lot in sets no longer being used, perhaps in the abandoned mine shaft or the haunted house.

Discuss what Parker would do now. He would probably develop a suspect list containing people who knew the suspect and might have had a motive for killing him.

5. A Suspect List

Explain that after further investigation, Detective Parker developed a list of suspects. Hand out the "Suspect List" (pages 55, 56 and 57). You can have all students read the list or designate seven students to be the suspects. Each suspect would then read the information regarding himself or herself to the class. The student detectives would be required to jot down significant facts about each person.

Discuss the suspects and their motives. Students will notice that they all have a motive.

Discuss what Detective Parker would do. In addition to a motive, the suspects would have to be able physically to impersonate Thornwell. Detective Parker would, therefore, gather facts regarding the suspects' physical characteristics.

6. Physical Characteristics

Hand out "Suspects' Physical Characteristics" (page 58). Ask students to examine and determine which suspects could have successfully impersonated Myrtle Thornwell based on their physical appearance. (Butch Bark, Veronica Blakemore, Diamond Star, Darnell Rowell, and Maverick West. Ivan Dovanich could not because of his weight and his beard. Stephanic Jonesburg could not because of his height and weight.)

6. Physical Evidence, continued

Tell students they can cross any suspect off the suspect list who physically could not impersonate Thornwell.

Discuss what Detective Parker would do now. In addition to a motive and the physical possibility of impersonating Thornwell, the suspects would have to be capable of the impersonation. Discuss what abilities would be required for this trickery ---- acting ability and ability to use make-up in such a way as to change one's appearance. Detective Parker would therefore consider which suspects would have these abilities. Discuss who would have this expertise. (Veronica Blakemore, Diamond Star, Darnell Rowell and Maverick West). Explain that Darnell is not an actress; however, because she is a professional make-up artist, she must be considered as a possible suspect.

Discuss what Detective Parker would do now. He would look for alibis.

7. Alibis

Hand out Parker's notes regarding the suspects' alibis (page 59). Have students read the detective's notes and complete their own notes. Discuss their ideas about the case so far.

Discuss what Detective Parker would do now. He would substantiate alibis. Ask students who could substantiate each alibi.

8. Alibis Substantiation

Hand out Parker's notes regarding the questioning to substantiate the alibis (page 60). Read the notes. Have students write their own notes and discuss them. They should be able to cross Veronica and Darnell off the list because they had substantiated alibis.

Discuss what Detective Parker would do now. He would search for more evidence.

9. A Make-Up Clue

Explain that Detective Parker was contacted by the forensic lab with new evidence.

Hand out Parker's notes regarding the make-up clue, (page 61). Read the notes about the clue and complete notes about the case so far. Discuss current developments. Students should conclude that Maverick can be scratched off of the suspect list.

Discuss what Detective Parker would do now. He would search for more evidence.

10. A Slip of the Tongue

Explain that Detective Parker got a new piece of evidence unexpectedly. A cameraman, filming the day of the crime, contacted him with what proved to be a crucial clue.

Hand out Parker's note regarding a slip of the tongue, (page 62). Read the new evidence and complete the notes about the case. Discuss how this slip of the tongue nailed the suspect. They should conclude that the clue revealed that the culprit was someone who had worked at the studio years ago and therefore knew the cameraman's nickname. The only one of the remaining suspects who had worked at the studio years ago was Diamond Star. Therefore, the murderer was Diamond.

Congratulate the class on a job well done. Review assumptions and discuss the need to continue gathering evidence until there is enough to support an arrest.

Read the Epilogue, (page 63).

A Hollywood Crime

Newspaper Article

Film Producer Killed

Storm Van Harsky, Hollywood's famed producer of three Academy Award winning films, including "Guilty," died Tuesday evening. His body was discovered by the night security guard on the set of his current movie at Van Horror Studios.

Van Harsky, age 64, was pronounced dead when police arrived at the scene at 9:00 p.m. An autopsy revealed Van Harsky was poisoned. Money found in the victim's wallet indicates that robbery was not the motive.

A lover of suspense, Van Harsky created Van Horror Studios in 1952. He has produced over 200 movies, each one well-known for its suspense and use of special effects.

Van Harsky had no survivors. Funeral arrangements are pending.

Detective Parker's Notes

Facts about the Case

- Van Harsky was currently producing the film, "Terrified." Production went as usual on the set the day of the crime. Work began at 5:30 a.m. and ended at 6:00 p.m. The set was cleared by 6:30 p.m. according to Fred Jones, the night security guard. Company policy required him to check the set after each day's shooting.
- The body was found in a castle on the back lot. The castle is located 50 yards west of a haunted house and 75 yards east of an abandoned mine shaft.

- All of the inside shots in the film are made inside this castle, not on a sound stage. This is true of most of Van Harsky's films. He constructs a whole building or structure, and uses the interior as well as the exterior. He was using one of the castle's turret rooms as his office.
- His secretary, Myrtle Thornwell, remained at his main office located near the studio entrance during the day. She came to his "castle" office, each evening after the day's shoot to discuss any business needing attention. She always brought him a pot of hot tea.
- No one entered the studio after 5:30 p.m. There is only one entrance to the studio. The studio is surrounded by a 14 foot cement wall. Two security guards are at the entrance gate 24 hours a day.

- One of the cameramen was talking with Fred Jones on the set. They both stated they saw Van Harsky go into the office at 6:15 p.m. The cameraman reported he had passed the secretary as she entered the castle on her way to Van Harsky's office around 6:20 p.m. She had several folders under one arm and was carrying a tray containing a tea pot and two cups. Other witnesses also reported seeing Thornwell going to Van Harsky's office.
- The night security guard made a routine check of the back lot at 8:30 p.m. Upon inspecting the castle, he noticed the door to Van Harsky's office was slightly ajar. He peeked in to investigate and found Van Harsky's body.

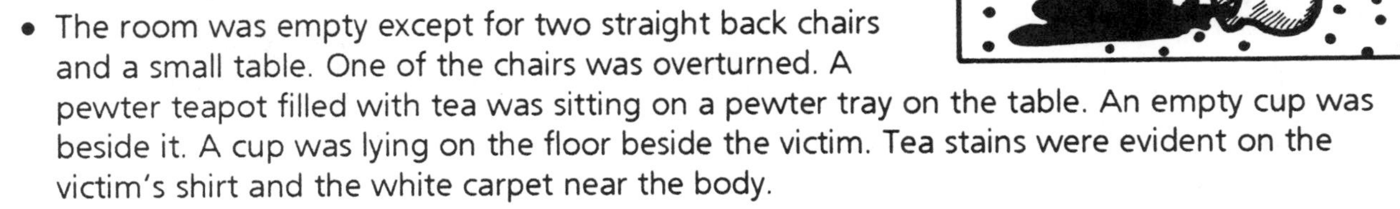

- The room was empty except for two straight back chairs and a small table. One of the chairs was overturned. A pewter teapot filled with tea was sitting on a pewter tray on the table. An empty cup was beside it. A cup was lying on the floor beside the victim. Tea stains were evident on the victim's shirt and the white carpet near the body.

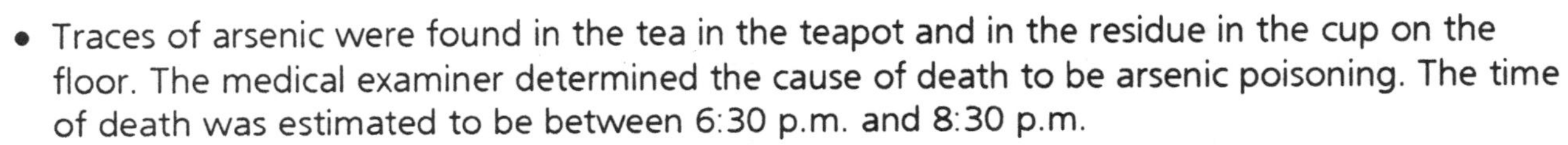

- Traces of arsenic were found in the tea in the teapot and in the residue in the cup on the floor. The medical examiner determined the cause of death to be arsenic poisoning. The time of death was estimated to be between 6:30 p.m. and 8:30 p.m.

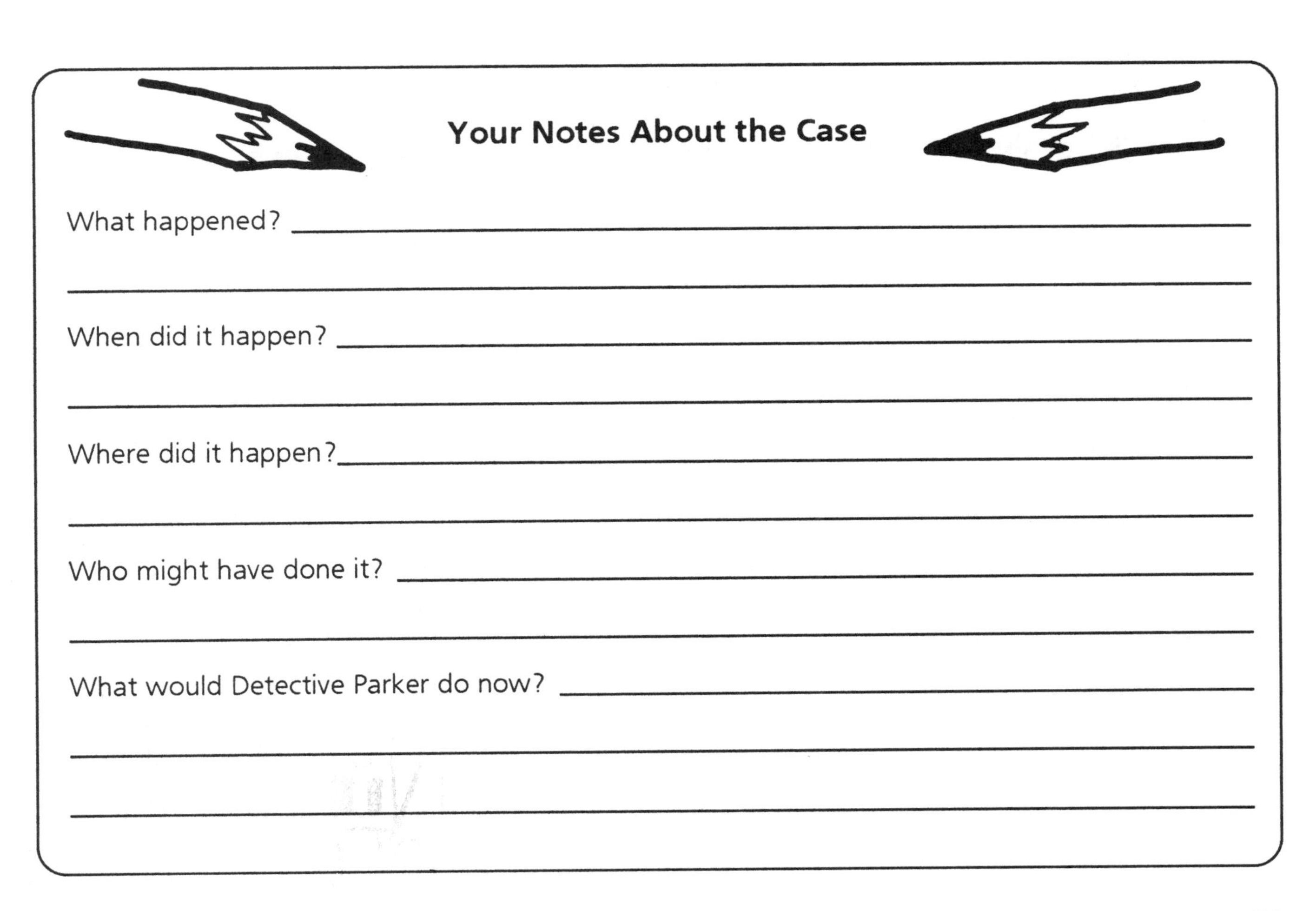

Your Notes About the Case

What happened? ____________________

____

When did it happen? ____________________

____

Where did it happen? ____________________

____

Who might have done it? ____________________

____

What would Detective Parker do now? ____________________

____

____

Detective Parker's Notes

Facts About Myrtle Thornwell

- Myrtle Thornwell - age 59 - Thornwell is a spinster who has worked for Van Harsky for 10 years. She was recently told that she must retire on her 60th birthday. She had pleaded with Van Harsky to allow her to work for ten more years in order to receive a better pension. He had refused.
- According to one of Thornwell's friends, he had told the secretary he needed someone younger, with more energy. Thornwell had said to another secretary, "It is not fair, after all my hard work and dedication. I hope he gets what he deserves."

Follow-up of Questioning of Myrtle Thornwell

- No one was at Thornwell's home when detectives went there for questioning at 10:30 p.m. the night of the crime. A neighbor said he saw her leave that morning around 8:30 a.m. and had not seen her since.
- "She was evidently in a hurry," he stated. "Didn't even say hello. Quite unlike her. She seemed to be nervous; upset or something."
- The guard at the studio gate reported seeing Myrtle enter the studio that morning. "Nine o'clock sharp, as usual," he said.
- A secretary for the studio's accountant reported seeing Myrtle go into her office a little after nine that morning. "I didn't see her all day," she said. "Which was unusual. She would frequently come to my office and get me for a morning or afternoon coffee break."

Your Notes About the Case

How might the crime have happened? ______________________________

____

Who might have done it? ______________________________

____

Why? ______________________________

____

What would Detective Parker do now? ______________________________

Detective Parker's Notes

Interview with Myrtle Thornwell

- Myrtle Thornwell returned to her home the evening after the crime.
- She stated that she had received a call at 9:00 p.m. Monday night, the night before the crime, from a nurse in Boston. The nurse told Myrtle that her brother, her only living relative, had suffered a stroke and was in the hospital. The nurse explained that they had found her name and number in his wallet.
- She called Van Harsky to tell him she was going to fly to Boston the next day. She said he wasn't home, so she left a message on his answering machine.
- She then made airline reservations for a flight the next morning, leaving Los Angeles at 9:45 a.m. and arriving in Boston at 7:00 p.m. She had a two-hour layover in Chicago.
- Upon arriving in Boston, she took a cab to the hospital but found that her brother had not been admitted. She called his home and found him there. He picked her up at the hospital. She flew back to Los Angeles the next day, Wednesday.

Your Notes About the Case

What would Detective Parker do now? ______________________________

____

____

Detective Parker's Notes

Facts to Substantiate Thornwell's Statement

- Alta Airlines reservations confirmed that Myrtle Thornwell was aboard their flight 192 to Boston on the day of the crime. She returned to Los Angeles on flight 63 on Wednesday, the day after the crime.
- Her brother in Boston stated that his sister had called him from the Boston hospital. "I was so surprised to know she was in Boston. It's still puzzling me why in the world she thought I was sick. Who could have called her?"
- When the woman at the hospital's information desk was shown Thornwell's picture, she reported, "She came to the desk, wanting to know her brother's room number. I distinctly remember because when I told her he hadn't been admitted, she got angry. You'd think she would have been relieved."
- When Van Harsky's housekeeper was questioned, she stated that her employer had been out the night before the crime. "I think he must have gotten in late and didn't bother to play his messages when he got in, because the next morning when I was bringing him his coffee, I heard him listening to them. One message was from his secretary saying something about an emergency in Boston and that she had to go out of town. There was another; a prank call, I think. It must have been some kids. Then the secretary called back, saying her brother was all right after all and she didn't need to make the trip and would be at work the next day."

- Van Harsky erased the messages. The housekeeper couldn't remember what time the calls had been made.

How does this information change your ideas about the case?

Your Notes About the Crime

Who? ______________________________

How? ______________________________

____

What would Detective Parker do now? ______________________________

____

The Suspects

Ivan Dovanich

Age 54. Dovanich has directed most of the victim's films. He is currently directing the movie, "Haunted Turret." He had been heard arguing with the victim over the length of time it was taking to complete the film. The movie was one billion dollars over budget. This was due to Dovanich's misuse of time and a "tired old eye," Van Harsky was heard saying. He had then threatened to cancel Dovanich's contract for the film, giving the director only one-half the previously agreed upon income from the film. After the threat, Dovanich had walked off the set. "Good riddance!" Van Harsky had exclaimed. "I've been waiting for an excuse to get new blood in this company!" Van Harsky had then hired a young director to finish the film.

Stephanic Jonesburg

Age 28. Jonesburg, a special effects technician, developed a new technique using holograms to make ghosts leap out from the screen into the audience. He had tried to get a patent on the technique but had found that a patent had already been issued under the name Hershey Petronelli. He later found out that Petronelli was Van Harsky's real name. Jonesburg had accused the victim of stealing the technique. Van Harsky had retaliated by firing him four days ago.

Butch Bark

Age 47. Bark had been a stunt man in most of Van Harsky's films. He was not, however, in the current movie. It was rumored that the victim had refused to hire Bark because he was "over the hill" for a stunt man. Bark had told an acquaintance that he had pleaded with Van Harsky to hire him. "He needed the money real bad," the acquaintance had said. It seems that Bark is a closet video game freak and spends all of his spare time playing video games. He has spent all of the money he had made in the movies on expensive games that he keeps in a video arcade he has built in his house.

Van Harsky was unsympathetic to Bark's pleas for work. "He knew the life of a stunt man was short," Van Harsky was heard saying. "He should have planned for this day instead of spending everything he made."

Veronica Blakemore

Age 20. Blakemore is a new starlet in Hollywood. She met the victim at a Hollywood party. Van Harsky promised to give her a screen test and even set up an appointment. Veronica came to the test with her cousin, also an actress. Van Harsky took one look at the cousin and immediately knew she was perfect for the leading role in "Haunted Turret." He hired her on the spot and sent Veronica away without even a glance, according to her cousin.

Veronica was reportedly bitter and had stated at a dinner party that she wished something evil would get him. "Like one of the famous Van Harsky demons," she was overheard saying.

Diamond Star

Age 67. Star is a former movie actress, star of many Van Harsky films. In the last movie she made twenty-five years ago, her character was supposed to be attacked by mice. Terrified of mice all her life, Star had refused to play a scene where five mice were to crawl on her unconscious body. Angered by her refusal, Van Harsky ordered her off the set, promised her she would never work in his studio or any other studio again. He had kept true to his word and had seen to it that she had never worked as an actress again.

The fortune she had made has dwindled to nothing. She is currently living in a low-rent apartment and works as a manicurist in a beauty salon. A customer stated that she constantly talks about her parts in old films. She remembers many of her lines from these movies and often speaks them as she is filing nails.

Darnell Rowell

Age 30. Rowell was a makeup artist who created faces for the vampires and other monsters for Van Harsky's films. She was fired eight months ago when working on the victim's last completed film, "The Vampire's Thin Blood." she had failed to make a vampire scary enough to suit Van Harsky. "This face looks like one you would see at a child's birthday party," he had screamed.

She was immediately barred from the studio. She has been too depressed since her firing to get another job. Made up like a ghoul, she has recently been spotted at the studio. Sympathetic to her situation, however, none of her friends who recognized her reported her to Van Harsky.

Maverick West

Age 70. West is one of the most famous villains ever in film. Though he has played in many of Van Harsky's films, he and the victim had never gotten along. It was rumored that West had always resented Van Harsky for type-casting him into the villain role. "He had always seen himself as the dashing leading man, another Clark Gable," a friend had stated. He was evidently having regrets about the way his career had turned out. "That Van Harsky cheated me out of what is rightly mine," he had recently stated to a reporter of a national tabloid. "What I should have is a nation of devoted fans; women dreaming of my incredible charm. Instead, I'm hated by all; considered more evil than the devil himself."

Your Notes About the Case

Who would have a motive? ______________________________

____

What suspects can be eliminated because they do not have motives? ______________________________

____

What would Detective Parker do now? ______________________________

____

Detective Parker's Notes

Suspects' Physical Characteristics

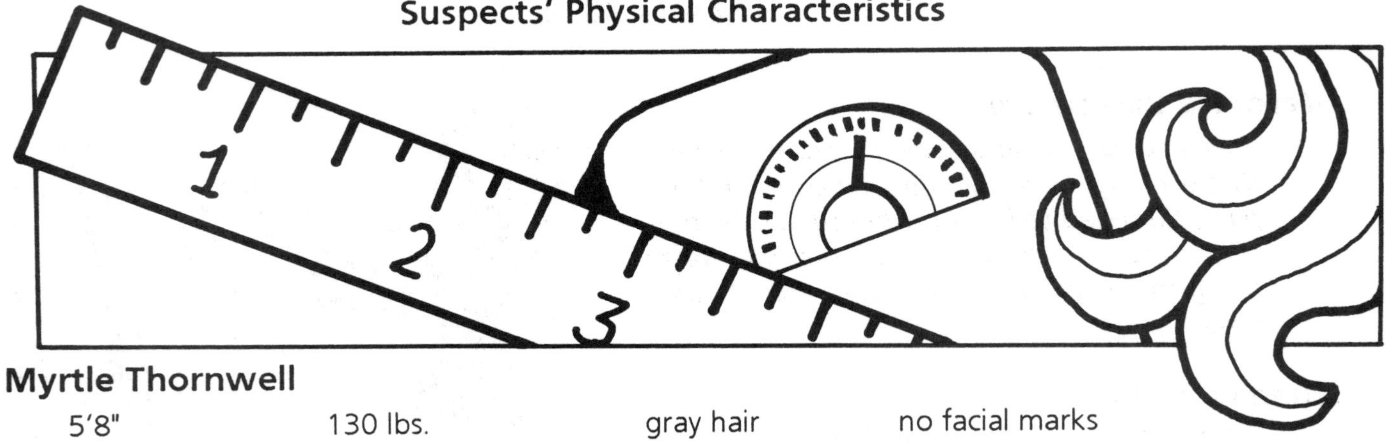

Name	Height	Weight	Hair	Facial marks
Myrtle Thornwell	5'8"	130 lbs.	gray hair	no facial marks
Ivan Dovanich	5'8-1/2"	220 lbs.	black hair	graying beard
Stephanic Jonesburg	6'2'	190 lbs.	brown hair	no facial marks
Butch Bark	5'8'	140 lbs.	brown hair	scar on left cheek
Veronica Blakemore	5'7-1/2"	125 lbs.	red hair	mole on right cheek bone
Diamond Star	5'8-1/2"	130 lbs.	blonde hair	no facial marks
Darnell Rowell	5'7-1/2"	132 lbs.	red hair	freckles
Maverick West	5'7-1/2"	145 lbs.	black hair	no facial marks

Your Notes About the Case

Who could physically impersonate Myrtle Thornwell? ______________________________

What expertise would be needed to impersonate Thornwell? ______________________________

____

Who would have this expertise? ______________________________

Detective Parker's Notes

Suspects' Alibis

Veronica Blakemore

"I was out shopping all day for a dress to wear that evening. I went to a dinner party at 7:00 p.m., but I had to leave my house at 6:00 p.m. It was about 45 minutes away, but with traffic being the way it always is, I gave myself more time."

Diamond Star

"I took the day off from the shop and went to Sunland Beach. I didn't get home until around 5:30 p.m. or so. Then I stretched out on the sofa and watched videos all evening."

Darnell Rowell

"That was the day I decided to take some action and do something with my life. I actually got up, got dressed and was at the personnel office at CSX Studios by 7:45 a.m."

"I waited for what seemed like hours but finally had an interview. I got a job. After that I called a friend and we met at Zelda's Restaurant to celebrate. We ended up going swimming at her apartment and had a pool-side dinner. I didn't get home until after 9:30."

Maverick West

"I was home all day and evening; all alone. Even my housekeeper wasn't there. It was her day off.

Your Notes About the Case

____

____

____

What would Detective Parker do now? ______________________

____

Detective Parker's Notes

Questioning to Substantiate Alibis

Veronica Blakemore

- The hostess stated that Veronica was the first guest to arrive. "She rang the doorbell at seven o'clock on the dot."

Diamond Star

- When shown Diamond's picture, none of the lifeguards at the beach that day remembered seeing Diamond.

Darnell Rowell

- The personnel director's secretary stated that she had seen Darnell that day. "She was at my office when I got there at 8:00 a.m., standing right outside the door. I let her in and she sat there for a long time. She didn't leave until around noon."
- Darnell's friend stated that Darnell had called her around 12:30 p.m. "She was so excited about a job and wanted to meet me to celebrate. We met at Zelda's then went back to my place for a swim. She didn't leave until almost nine."

Your Notes About the Case

____

____

Who has an alibi? ______________________________

What would Detective Parker do now? ______________________

____

Detective Parker's Notes

A Clue Involving Make-up

Make-up was found on the victim's shirt. It was taken to the lab and analyzed.

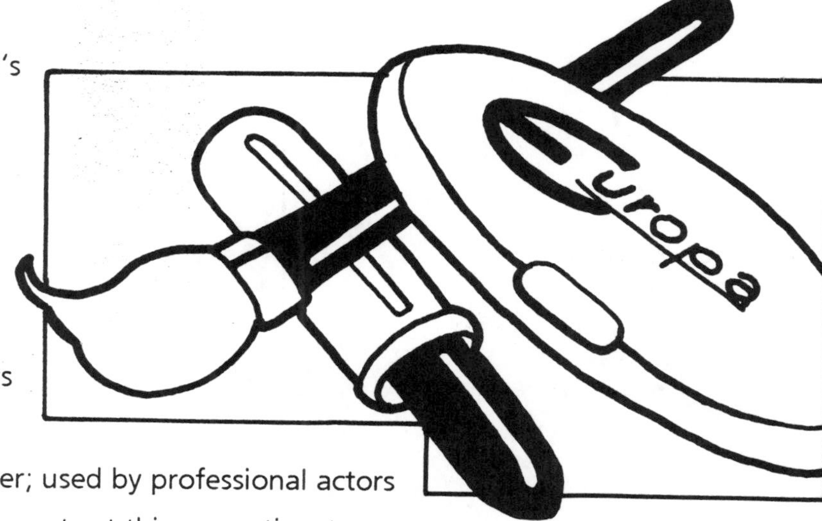

Facts about the make-up:

- alcohol based
- made by Europa Cosmetics
- sold at Look Beautiful Cosmetics Company in Hollywood
- a make-up designed for full cover; used by professional actors
- Diamond and Veronica have accounts at this cosmetics store

Additional Facts:

- Both women had recently purchased this type of foundation make-up at the store but the store had no record of what shade they bought.
- Store records showed that Maverick often bought hair dye at the store but he had never purchased make-up.

Your Notes About the Case

____

____

Who would have access to the make-up found on the victim? ____________________

____

How do you know? ______________________________________

____

What would Detective Parker do now? ____________________________

____

Detective Parker's Notes

A Clue Involving a Slip of the Tongue

- Eastman Davis, a veteran cameraman and Van Harsky's favorite camera operator, called today to state that he remembered something that happened on the day of the crime.
- "I had just finished getting everything ready for the next day's shoot and was leaving the castle. I passed Myrtle who was carrying tea to Van Harsky. I nodded to her. She nodded back and said, 'Hi Lenscap.' That was my nickname years ago before Myrtle started working here. I didn't think anything about it at the time; but I started wondering, why she would have said that. Anyway, I thought it wouldn't hurt to tell you."

Your Notes About the Case

Who is guilty? ______________________________

How do you know? ______________________________

____

____

____

Epilogue

A warrant was issued for Diamond Star's arrest. At the police station where she was questioned after the arrest, she confessed to everything. Her statement reads as follows:

"I have planned this for a long time; years to be exact. Late at night after watching the videos of my old movies, I would lie in bed plotting until I fell asleep.

About a month ago, a costume designer for Van Harsky, came into my shop for a manicure. She was surprised to find me there, painting a customer's nails. It hurt me deeply to see her pitiful stare. I knew what she was thinking; that I should be the one receiving that service. Me, the great star, should never have been put in the position in which she found me.

I swallowed my pride and when she sat down at my table, I casually asked questions about the studio. It was then that I learned about the new movie. I had always known that Van Harsky closed his day with a cup of tea. He's done that for years. And now, I had a plan. What a perfect setting for his demise, the turret room in the castle. Quite fitting for the King of Horror.

I called Myrtle Thornwell several times, pretending to be taking a survey. That way I could hear her voice. I taped these conversations and perfected her speech.

The day of the crime was my final, yet best performance.

Diamond was convicted. Serving time changed Diamond. She began a drama class for inmates and formed an actor's troupe. They have received recognition for their fine performances. Several inmates received parole and are currently working in television, one of them on a day-time soap opera.

Summary of Mysteries

A Mystery at the Mall

Molly - Oswald, D-, 3:30 p.m. 10 minutes, 5'1", red hair, blue coat, green plaid shirt

Otis - Snodgrass, F-, 3:10 p.m. 30 minutes, 5"10", brown hair, yellow coat, brown shirt

Norman - Mitchell, D, 3:15 p.m., 20 minutes, 5'5", black hair, tan trench coat, orange sweatshirt

Samantha - Nelson, C, 3:25 p.m., 15 minutes, 4'8", blonde hair, red jacket, white shirt

Students compare the descriptions of the suspects with the descriptions of the people that were seen by the witnesses at the mall. From this they can conclude that Otis stole the cookie.

The Coaster Caper

Roscoe Hepplewhite - eliminated in lesson 2 with the Suspect List because he had no motive

Earline Felldown - eliminated in lesson 4 with "Physical Evidence" because she would not be able to fit the clothing

Benny Berleine - the guilty person

Arnold Winall - eliminated in lesson 5 because his shoe does not match the print left at the crime scene

Mildred Kerkel - eliminated in lesson 5 because she does not have blonde hair

Melody Voice - eliminated in lesson 3 because she had an alibi that could be substantiated

The Case of Santa's Blackmail

Mistletoe Kisses - eliminated in lesson 4 with the "Newspaper Clue" because she still had the two papers in her cellar

Caroling Noel - eliminated in lesson 2 because she had no motive. This is reinforced in lesson 3 when her prints are not found on the door

Yuley Gooch - the guilty person

Tinsel Green - eliminated in lesson 3 with information about the fingerprints

Curley Bows - eliminated in lesson 4 because he never buys a newspaper

Merry Bells - eliminated in lesson 5 with the chromatography test

The Case of the Missing Tiara

Theodore Hobson (manager) - eliminated in lesson 2 because he had no motive and in lesson 3 because he had an alibi

Mary Bell Brimstone (day desk clerk) - eliminated in lesson 4 when the powder from the crime scene didn't match the powder found on her shoes

Brevard Meldane (night desk clerk) - the guilty person

Nelson Painter (night security guard) - eliminated in lesson 2 because he had no motive and in lesson 3 because he had an alibi that was substantiated

Justin Aber (chef) - eliminated in lesson 5 with the typewriter clue

Natasha McNeeley (penthouse maid) - eliminated in lesson 3 because she had an alibi that could be substantiated

A Hollywood Crime

Myrtle Thornwell - the information in lesson 4 substantiated her story and established the fact that she was out of town at the time of the crime

Ivan Dovanich - eliminated in lesson 6 because his physical characteristics mean that he could not impersonate the secretary

Stephanic Jonesburg - eliminated in lesson 6 because his physical characteristics mean that he could not impersonate the secretary

Butch Bark - eliminated in lesson 6 because he lacked the skills necessary to be able to impersonate the secretary

Veronica Blakemore - eliminated in lesson 8 because she had a valid alibi

Diamond Star - guilty; the information about the make-up and the slip of the tongue point to her as the guilty person

Darnell Rowell - eliminated in lesson 8 because he had an alibi that could be substantiated

Maverick West - Eliminated in lesson 9 with the make-up clue